Making Kid Time Count

for Ages 0–3

The Attentive Parent Advantage

Sarahlynne Davis, EdM

I'm so happy you could come & have met you! Sarah

Lesson Ladder
Success within reach!

www.lessonladder.com

21 Orient Street, Melrose, MA 02176

XAMonline, Inc., Melrose, MA 02176

This book is intended to educate and provide general information about caring for your young child. This book should not, however, be construed to dispense medical services or be used to diagnose or treat any medical condition. All questions and decisions about your child and his/her medical care should be addressed directly with a qualified health-care professional, including your child's pediatrician. Accordingly, you are encouraged to consult your personal health-care provider before adopting any of the suggestions in this book or drawing inferences from it.

While the author, editor and publisher have endeavored to prepare an accurate and helpful book, they make no representations or warranties, express or implied, with respect to the accuracy or completeness of its contents and specifically disclaim any warranties of merchantability or fitness for a particular purpose. The author, editor and publisher do not assume and hereby disclaim any liability to any party for any loss, damage or injury caused, directly or indirectly, by any error, omission or information provided in this book.

The names, conditions and identifying details of people associated with the events and advice described in this book have been changed to protect their privacy. Any similarities to actual individuals are merely coincidental.

Published 2013
Printed in the United States
1 2 3 4 5 6 7 13 12 11 10 09 08

Lesson Ladder: an imprint of XAMonline, Inc.
21 Orient Street, Melrose, MA 02176

Toll Free: 1-800-301-4647
Fax: 1-617-583-5552
Email: customerservice@lessonladder.com
Web: www.lessonladder.com

Text: **Sarahlynne Davis, EdM**
Illustrations: Angela Montoya, Rachel Enos, Terrie Cundiff
Front cover: ThinkStock/86501132
Back cover: ThinkStock/118849440
Author photo credit: CA Smith Photography
Book design: iiCREATIVE
Production: nSight, Inc.
Project management: Elizabeth St. Germain
Acquisitions editor: Beth Kaufman

Library of Congress Catalog Card Number:
(pending)
Sarahlynne Davis, EdM
Making Kid Time Count for Ages 0–3 206 pp., ill.

1. Title
2. Parenting
3. Toddlers–Handbooks, manuals, etc.
4. Child development
5. Parent-child relations
6. Early childhood development
7. Language development.

HQ774.5 D38 2013 649.122 D2611 2013
ISBN: 978-098-486-5789

Dedication

I dedicate this book to my two beautiful sweethearts, my children, Kyler and Aurelia. There will never be enough snuggles, enough laughter, or enough time with you.

And because we are all children first, I dedicate this book to my parents, who have always made me feel like the most important person, and who always listen to what I have to say.

Acknowledgements

First of all, I have to thank my best friend, and most amazing and extremely understanding husband. His continuous enthusiasm and excitement for this project has been incredibly motivating, and I can't thank him enough for his patience when most nights I said, "I'm going to write," instead of, "Sure, I'll watch a movie with you." All my love!

And a special thank you to my inspirations, my children: To my son, Kyler, a kindhearted little boy who makes me laugh all the time. And to my newest sweetheart, my beautiful daughter, Aurelia. What a cheerful and sweet snuggle bunny you are! I feel so blessed and thankful for such a loving family.

I want to especially thank the fantastic team at Lesson Ladder, and most especially, my incredible editor, Beth Kaufman. From the beginning, her endless enthusiasm, incredible care, and positive support have been instrumental in the process of writing this book. I couldn't have asked for a better person to guide me through this last year. I'm extraordinarily thankful to Lesson Ladder, including Sharon Wynne, for giving me this most remarkable opportunity to author this book.

This book was blessed with a few amazing editors. Developmental editor Corbin Lewars's comments and support brought the book to a whole new level. Dr. Betty Bardige was instrumental in helping to include the most recent and cutting-edge parenting research. Dr. Sylvia Sirignano's comments added excellent insight to the nuances of the book. Finally, Meera Dash's incredible talents tied the chapters all together, making the book flow together seamlessly.

This book wouldn't have been possible without the amazing contributors: the parents, grandparents, Evanthia Granville, MEd, co-creator of merelymothers.com, and professionals who generously provided inspiring activities for young children. I am in awe of your creativity! Thank you: Dr. Patricia Wynne, mother of two; Kate Delaney Bailey, occupational therapist and mother of two; Bonnie Brown, Suzuki instructor; Anne D., preschool educator, grandmother, and mother of three; Dawn D., mother of two; Marc D., father of two; Mary G., mother of two; Neal G., father of two; Alison H., MPH, mother of three; Marissa H., mother of three; Eric and Geeta L., physicians and parents of two; Liz Rogers, preschool educator and mother of two; and Rebecca Irwin Slater, MA, elementary education/multiple subject credential.

About the Author

Sarahlynne Davis, EdM, is an experienced educator who has taught in public, private, and charter schools. She has had the privilege of writing curriculum, teaching, and mentoring at a variety of levels, from kindergarten through eighth grade. Her specialties include literacy and writing skills, especially with students who struggle with conceptual understanding of reading strategies. She has been trained in research-based, systematic reading programs. Her formal education includes a master of education in literacy from the University of San Diego, a language arts teaching credential from Indiana Wesleyan University, literacy training at the Dyslexia Institute of Indiana, and a bachelor's degree in English and government from Skidmore College. She is currently pursuing a doctorate of education at Texas A&M University.

A passionate parenting guru, Sarahlynne has written for *Z-Life* magazine, *Shine, Yahoo!*, and a variety of online publications. She is also a co-creator of merelymothers.com, a website that encourages conversation about all aspects of motherhood, from philosophies to fashion.

Sarahlynne lives in Virginia with her husband and two young children, who were the inspiration for this book!

Contents

Chapter 6: The Basics of Play: Why, Where, When, and How

Chapter 7: Creative Play: Setting the Stage for Success

Chapter 8: Exploring Nature and the Community with Your Baby

9

Chapter 9: The Consequences of Screen Time

10

Chapter 10: Preparing Your Family for Another Child

Introduction

It's 5:30 in the evening. If I'm lucky, I've already made dinner, because from 5:30 to about 8:00, I'm bouncing back and forth between my children. My two-year-old son needs to eat, my infant daughter needs to nurse, both of them need a bath, my son inevitably wants me to help him build a tower or race his cars around the kitchen floor, and my daughter wants to be rocked and snuggled. My husband usually gets home in the middle of the chaos, and we tag-team until both children are asleep, usually at about 9:30, much later than we planned.

But each day, when my daughter wakes up from her early evening nap, I optimistically begin her bath, hoping that tonight, my husband and I will succeed in getting the children fed, bathed, and in bed early. My son is usually engrossed in play in the other room during this time, and unless he asks to help, I don't interrupt him. His sister's bath goes quickly, and until a few days ago, I didn't think my busy toddler even noticed. But then the other day he brought out a plastic container and put his baby doll, Max, inside. After fetching a facecloth from the bathroom, he gently patted Max's body. A few minutes later he pulled Max out of the container, laid him down on a towel, and wrapped him up gently. "Baby has bathroom!" he proclaimed proudly.

Watching my son act out this scene, a scene that I didn't think he was even paying attention to, made me wonder: *If he can copy my actions so precisely when I don't even think he's looking, what else is he absorbing?*

The answer is *everything*. Everything from the way you order lunch to the way you talk to your spouse to how you lock the front door.

So many cognitive, social, and emotional connections are created during these first few years. They form a key developmental time in your baby's life and in your journey as a parent. The day you bring your baby home, you know very little about how you will parent, but as your child grows, you learn. You become more comfortable and confident. You make decisions that may seem trivial but will affect your child for years to come.

"He won't remember these days," some people say. That's probably true. Your child won't remember how he spent each day in his first few years. And actually, that's probably a good thing, because being an infant and toddler can be extremely frustrating! But the experiences he has now create the person he will become. The relationship you form with him now will lay the groundwork for how he communicates with you as an adolescent, teen, and adult. What qualities do you want to see in your child as he grows? What experiences can you give him to help him grow into the kind, generous, and positive person you envision?

Making Time for Your Baby

The best thing you can give to your child is your undivided attention. Not all the time, of course! It's quality, not quantity, that counts. For a certain amount of time each day, you have to be there, on the floor and in his world. He doesn't want or need a ton of toys, technological devices, or expensive experiences. Too many of these things can actually be detrimental to your child's development. He just wants you. He wants a walk outside to look at nature. He wants you to read as many books as he desires. He wants you to help him throw a ball, make a tower, spin in a circle and fall down laughing, or color a picture.

Sometimes giving kids undivided attention is incredibly difficult. We have to go to work, cook dinner, or do housework, or we have more than one child who needs us. So we put it off or tell our children, "Five more minutes." And then we find that they are playing well by themselves, so instead of following up on our promise to play, we proceed to our next task.

But when we do this, our children learn not to rely on us. A young child translates this into, "My mom doesn't always mean what she says." For an older child, that could become, "I can't tell my mom anything because she doesn't have time to listen." Attentive parenting is about respect; respect your child and respect yourself, and your relationship will blossom from this foundation of mutual admiration and trust. We have to be true to our word. If we say "Five more minutes," then in five minutes, or when we've finished our task, we should give our child our attention. It's only fair, and it teaches our child that they can trust us—with anything.

Whether you're a stay-at-home parent or you work outside the home, this book will show you what your infant and toddler really needs from you, how you can give him what he needs, and how you can feel good about the time you spend with him. If you have one hour a day with your child or twelve, this book will show you how to make your time with your kid count.

How This Book Was Born

Many early childhood books discuss cognitive and brain developmental research but don't explain what parents can do to help their child succeed in the major developmental milestones during the first few years. You may read a book on cognitive development for infants and toddlers and think, "How do I help my child make those great strides? What can I do for her?"

Other books offer plenty of resources, games, and activities to do with your baby. Those books, however, often don't discuss the whys behind the activities. The research component is missing.

So, when developing this book, we matched the most critical, latest research with parent-tested and teacher-tested activities. When you complete a game or activity with your child, you should know why you're doing it and how it will help your child grow and thrive.

The organization of this book

As a parent of young children, you probably have little time for reading, so this book is divided into 10 succinct chapters. The first half of the book takes you through the major, interrelated domains of development for an infant and toddler, including her need for bonding as well as cognitive, physical, sensory, language, and social development. Because the domains of development are so closely related, it's not practical to keep a strict sequence, but, roughly, the second half of the book focuses on additional vital areas, including literacy, creative arts, music, nature, community, television, and the introduction of a sibling. These later chapters reflect value choices, since parents will choose to focus on different areas. This is how a child will grow up to be like her parents, learn more about whatever it is the parents find valuable, and become a member of the parents' specific culture and family background. All chapters provide you with activities to help your child along in each of these domains and areas.

What you'll find in each chapter

The first half of every chapter is dedicated to the whys: the research behind the activities and games listed in the second half of the chapter. (For easier reading, the notes citing the research appear near the end of the book.) Most chapters feature at least 10 to 20 research-based activities or games that you can play with your infant and toddler. All of these activities have been tested by parents, teachers, or both.

The activity portion of a chapter is usually divided into two sections. The first section lists activities for an infant's first year and the second section is for toddlers from one to three years old. You'll notice that the infant activities are simple and require little or no preparation. Infants love everything; the whole world is brand new, so you don't need elaborate activities to keep their attention. The more complicated activities in each chapter allow for the cognitive and emotional development of your growing child, an older toddler who is looking to explore the world in a more intricate way.

Many of these activities are perfect when you have five minutes of downtime or are in a transitional moment with your baby. Fight the urge to check your phone (I am SO guilty of this!) and try one of the suggested fast and fun techniques instead. The suggested activities are just that: suggestions. Do the ones that feel natural to you and your parenting style. And remember, sometimes allowing your child to lead you into their game is just as, if not more, important than incorporating your agendas.

The chapters are meant to be read as separate entities, but they also flow together to make a whole. Feel free to flip to your preferred section, or read the book cover to cover. Whatever you choose, this book will show you how to make the time you have with your baby really count. It's not difficult, but it's not always obvious, and the research is going to astound you.

Letting Go of the Guilt and Taking Care of Yourself

Okay, confession time. Parenting is hard. And it's messy. Some days we feel like rock stars, and other days we feel like we did everything wrong. Some days we wonder where our patience went and we count the minutes to bedtime. And there are other days when we wonder, "Am I enough? Am I giving my child enough of my time and energy? Is my child happy?" We all have those days. I know. I've been there.

So, before you start reading, know that this book is not about the guilt. We all have too much of that already. It's about knowing how you can best spend time with your children, but also learning how to make parenthood an enjoyable and rewarding experience for both you and your little ones. Like any relationship, the parent–child relationship takes two people who are both happy and fulfilled. We often forget about that, since we spend so much time caring for our babies. But what we're really doing is developing one of the most important and rewarding relationships we'll ever have.

In order to do that, we have to take care of our babies as well as ourselves. While you're reading this book and prioritizing time for your child, keep in mind that your needs and your marriage's needs are important too and need to be prioritized as well. And please know that it's completely normal to feel as though you don't have enough time for yourself and your partner! Actually, many couples find that adding a child to their family causes many significant, and often initially negative impacts as they learn to rediscover their new family unit and the roles everyone will play.

But taking care of yourself and your marriage is a huge key to your success and happiness as a parent and, believe it or not, your baby's development! More than 80% of couples experience a huge drop in marital quality during the transition to parenthood. Studies have also shown that infants as young as six months can experience increased blood pressure, heart rate, and stress hormones and be less able to respond to new stimuli and calm themselves when consistent marital conflict is present in the home. These effects can create children who may become antisocial and aggressive in later childhood. We all fight with our partners, so don't worry if your child observes the occasional argument. What he should also observe, however, is the reconciliation. Hug and say you're sorry in front of your baby, allowing him to see how these heated discussions are resolved. This teaches your child the positive effects of arguing: that both sides can see what is upsetting the other, apologize, and try to change.

So, even though your world revolves around your children, make an effort to nurture yourself and your marriage. This could be as simple as going for a run, taking a bath, or hiring a babysitter once a month and going on a date with your spouse. And keep your own cup full by finding someone to talk to about the successes and challenges of parenthood. Making time for these things can seem so difficult, and at times, when we're in the trenches of parenting young children, almost impossible, but taking care of ourselves is so incredibly important for everyone involved.

You should also keep in mind that you know your baby better than anybody else. After reading the advice of experts, only you can decide what's best for him. And remember to be easy on yourself. As parents, we learn every day. And every day is a new chance to start over.

I'm thrilled you've chosen this book to help you with your parenting journey. My hope is that after reading, you'll become a better parent than you already are and be more confident with the choices you make as a caregiver and as your child's first and most important teacher.

–Sarahlynne

Look for these bonus sections in every chapter!

A Tip from Sarahlynne

Bedtime Tricks and Techniques

- **Start with soft toys.** Give your child a stuffed animal to snuggle with, a pacifier, or a few toys to play with as she becomes sleepy.

Tips from Sarahlynne:

Need some out-of-the box answers on how to handle those daily and sometimes super frustrating infant and toddler challenges? Check out the Tips from Sarahlynne box!

What NOW?

Books to Help You Understand Your Baby's Temperament

- *The Happiest Baby on the Block* by Harvey Karp, M.D.

What Now?

From books to music to available classes for your little one, the "What Now?" box has your next step.

Making Kid Time Count

for Ages 0–3

Chapter Preview

- How to help your infant or toddler thrive
- Cognitive development in infants and toddlers
- Emotional needs of infants and toddlers
- What infants and toddlers need from their caregivers
- What quality time really means

Chapter 1

Ages 0–3: A Critical Time in Your Baby's Development

I live in the Washington, DC, area. Like many metropolitan areas, it is full of amazing wonders for a child intrigued by transportation and vehicles. In fact, my son's first sentence was, "Bye, bus!" as he waved to one of the public buses rumbling down the street. By the time he was two, I was used to him pointing out vehicles as they drove by. Even if he didn't know the correct words, he could point out a bus, a car, a train, and a truck.

One day, we were driving through one of the many little tunnels in our area. Normally, my son would just sit in silence through the tunnel, waiting for the sunlight to reappear. But this particular morning, he pointed to the surrounding darkness and exclaimed, "Car! Tunnel!"

"Yes! We are driving through a tunnel!" I could barely contain my excitement, and glancing back at him, I realized he couldn't either. He was laughing, pointing all around us, repeating, "Car! Tunnel!" And I was laughing with him.

We were both in this incredible moment of discovery, a quick minute of perfection and innocence.

And how quick it was. Seconds later, we were out of the tunnel, and my son was on to something else. (Such is the mind of a two-year-old.) But I wanted to hang onto that flawless moment; his pride and enthusiasm was just such a sweet and pure pause of time.

As parents, we want to hold onto all of these special times when we watch our children make new cognitive and emotional connections. But we can't; these discoveries are over so fast. And although we're thrilled and amazed by our children, they have no idea that what they've done is so incredible, so they move on, and we just have to hurry along and catch up.

Infants and toddlers are constantly absorbing what they see and developing new skills from each one of their interactions. These observations and connections help form a child's personality, teach him how to look at the world, and show him how to socialize with others and handle successes and failures. Your role as a parent is key to these interactions. Your reactions to his discoveries, frustrations, and successes all set the stage for his cognitive, social, and emotional development. We know when we welcome children into the world that our role is going to be tremendous, and as new parents, we may wonder: How can I give my child the best opportunities for growth? What are the most important things I can do for him to ensure that he's well adjusted, happy, and developmentally on track?

What Will Give Your Baby the Best Start in Life?

What are the first three years all about? It's relatively simple, but success is in the details. Let's delve into three major concepts that will help inform us throughout the next 10 chapters: relationships, environment, and experiences.

Relationships

We all know that our babies need one or two supportive and consistent caregivers in their lives to provide stability and self-confidence. But a strong and reliable caregiver–child relationship during the first few years can do much more than that. According to child development experts, the advantages include "sound mental health, motivation to learn, the ability to control aggressive impulses and resolve conflicts in nonviolent ways, knowing the difference between right and wrong, having the capacity to develop and sustain casual friendships and intimate relationships, and ultimately to be a successful parent oneself." Regardless of a family's situation, parents need to make sure that the consistent people in the child's life are loving, kind, and respectful of his many developmental needs. But what can a caregiver specifically do to be sure that these advantages are available to a child? What does a "strong and reliable caregiver" actually mean?

Environment

As important as a caregiver–child relationship is, a child's environment is just as critical. A good environment allows for a parent to give the child space to explore new and challenging skills but also step in to aid the child when necessary so that he doesn't get too frustrated. Eventually the child gains the confidence to complete new skills on his own. Environments that are predictable, are consistent, and allow for this kind of intervention aid in a child's "executive function" (ability to solve problems, complete tasks, and organize information) and teach children how to control their impulses and engage in "goal-directed behavior." So what exactly can caregivers do to create a predictable and consistent environment? What are the physical and emotional stages our children go through, and how can we use those stages as springboards for creating the safest and warmest environment?

Experiences

Your child's experience in his environment and with his caregiver sets the stage for how his predetermined genes are used, positively or negatively. First, as the research suggests, "Effective interventions can literally alter how children's genes work and, thereby, have long-lasting effects on their mental and physical health, learning, and behavior."

Secondly, children store newly learned information in the hippocampus within the temporal lobe, the part of the brain that stores and memorizes new information. When a child experiences something new, the hippocampus puts all the information into a "file cabinet" for later retrieval, creating what educators call a *background schema*. When the child is then put in a novel situation similar to one he's already faced, he'll automatically pull any information from these files that will help him navigate the new environment. So which activities should we prioritize with our infants and toddlers? How can we help them to internalize new experiences so that they create strong background schemas for the future?

Attentive parenting

The concepts of relationships, environment, and experiences should be in the back of your mind whenever you make a decision about how you're raising your child. All of his interactions and developments are related; his social development will affect his language, his language will affect his ability to play and bond, and so on.

A baby learns by observation and interaction. He becomes what he sees. There are people who will tell you that the first few years are not extraordinary, that the "kids won't remember anyway," so you can be lax with your time and your attention.

They couldn't be more wrong. According to experts, building an early, secure attachment will "contribute to the growth of a broad range of competencies, including a love of learning, a comfortable sense of oneself, positive social skills, multiple successful relationships at later ages, and a sophisticated understanding of emotions, commitment, morality, and other aspects of human relationships."

Building an early, secure attachment with your child will keep your relationship healthy for future years.

During the first years of a child's life, he'll make decisions, interact with others, and set expectations and priorities for himself. These are the years before school, before social pressures, and before the outside world tries to take over. During this short span, you have the opportunity to build a trusting, respectful bond with your child, a bond that will keep your relationship open and healthy for future years. If you're there for him when he's little, he'll be much more likely to let you in when he's older.

You've already begun this journey. But how can you understand your little one even better? How can you make your bond with him even stronger? We can begin to find answers by seeing how a baby's brain develops.

How Your Baby's Brain Processes Information

Did you know that intelligence is shaped after birth? Of course, genetics play a role, but recent brain research argues that consistent environmental factors can develop predisposed genes in a positive or negative way. That is, "We are born with the *potential* to develop these capacities—or not—depending on our experiences during infancy, throughout childhood, and into adolescence." What makes it easier to develop these capacities? Let's take a look at what happens inside a baby's brain during the first few years of life.

An infant's brain

When a baby is born, his brain is a quarter of its adult size. He has 100 billion neurons (nerve cells), but they're poorly connected. The consistent experiences he has will develop these connections into a network called a *circuitry*.

By his second birthday, his brain will have grown to three-quarters of its adult size, and it will be almost completely grown by the age of five. So, during the first two years of life, a baby is working overtime to understand and process new information. The neurons in his brain are made up of two kinds of fibers, *axons* and *dendrites*. Axons send messages to other neurons, and dendrites receive the messages. Every time your baby has a new experience, neurotransmitters send messages and make connections, or synapses, to other neurons. Each neuron is connected to thousands of others, and more synapses develop over time. At birth, a neuron has 2,500 synapses, but by the age of two or three, that number has increased to 15,000.

An infant's initial task is to survive, so all of his brain's connections are created with this purpose. This is why children born in so many different environments not only survive but thrive. A baby has many experiences, some that are consistently repeated and others that are not. Eventually, the brain lets go of connections that are not used as often and keeps the synapses used more often. This process is called *neural pruning*.

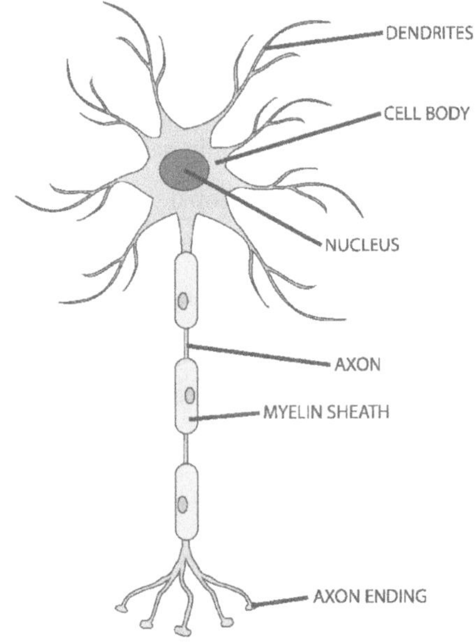

Neurons (nerve cells) work overtime in a baby's brain.

While a child's brain is learning which connections are important, a critical process called *myelination* is also happening frequently. Myelination occurs when the axons are surrounded by fat cells, which insulate the axons, allowing the impulses to travel faster and more efficiently. Myelination is how the nerve cells in the brain learn how to convey useful information quickly, allowing for the more complicated brain processes to take place. It occurs when the brain is improving or learning new cognitive or physical abilities—all the time in a young child. In fact, although myelination continues throughout a person's life, it happens most often during the first three years.

This means that the first years are crucial. A parent has the opportunity to give her child consistent experiences that he'll need and use throughout his life. During these first few years, a child learns how to absorb all the new stimuli, compartmentalize them, and use them again later. This skill will be used millions of times in a person's life, and it develops while the child grows from an infant to a toddler.

Rapid change during the early years

The various parts of a baby's brain are growing and changing all the time. For example, you may know that a newborn sees only 8 to 10 inches in front of him. However, by six to eight months, a baby's occipital lobe (the area of the brain that controls vision) is almost fully developed, and his eyes can see far and clear.

Another system that develops rather quickly is the baby's limbic system, where he processes emotional information. This is why it's so important to give your child plenty of attention and keep him safe and secure during the first few years. Research has shown that these emotional centers can be underdeveloped if a child is neglected or abused in these early years. Extensive neglect or abuse can have long-term negative effects in cognitive function and academic success, as well as emotional scarring such as trust issues, anxiety, and high stress. Conversely, research has also shown that if a baby feels safe and secure in his environment, he will perform better in cognitive tasks and have better academic success. It makes sense. If a child hasn't had his basic needs met, he cannot focus on learning anything else, because he's constantly making sure that, first and foremost, he's out of danger.

As parents, we already worry that we're not doing enough for our children's development, and now we have this additional pressure! But we can't always provide our children with undivided attention and uninterrupted care. So don't worry about the times you couldn't pick up your child the second he cried. The key here is *consistency.* Your baby will learn to process and hold onto the type of information that's available to him repeatedly over his early years. He'll let go of the rest.

What is your baby learning?

During these first few years, a baby is also learning how to store all of these consistent experiences so he can use them in future, unfamiliar situations. As parents, we can assist.

Background schema: When we play with and react to our children, we're helping them develop background schema, the "filing cabinet" that was mentioned earlier in this chapter. Background schema, also known as "crystallized intelligence," refers to how a child will use his background knowledge to understand, solve problems, and adapt to new situations.

The connections that children make as infants and toddlers turn into experiences that they pull from as older children when they're faced with a new challenge or situation, but only if their parents have helped them to make these connections. For example, a baby is crying in his bouncy chair, and after a few moments, his mother or father comes to pick him up. He feels heard, secure, and happy. Consequently, when he cries at night, he calms himself by remembering that when he cried during the day, someone acknowledged him. If someone now comes to him within a short amount of time, he's reassured that this behavior will elicit this same, consistent response from his caregiver. But if no one arrives, he's left confused. Why did someone comfort him this afternoon but not now, when it's dark?

Try to be consistent so that your child learns what will and will not happen in common situations. If the parent isn't consistent in his responses, the child won't be able to access any previously gained knowledge and may feel full of anxiety in a new situation. Conversely, if your child can predict how you will react and knows you will attend to his needs, he'll be much more easygoing, calm, and easy to please.

Metacognition: Background schema refers not just to new emotional experiences but also to new cognitive and intellectual tasks, such as puzzles, games, crafts, and activities. Parents should access a child's previous knowledge whenever they can. When they do, they're helping their child to become *metacognitive*, which means that the child can "think about thinking." A metacognitive person knows what his capabilities are, and when he looks at solving a problem, understands which strategy will be the most efficient and useful. Of course, your young child will not be independently metacognitive until he is older. But if you set the stage now, you can help your child become comfortable solving problems on his own with minimal frustration. See the sidebar for some tips and tricks for helping your little one to become metacognitive.

Eventually (and this could take years!) your baby will become very comfortable with this process. But during those first few years of life, he needs to be reminded how to pull from his previous experiences and use them to help him understand new ones. Remember that as you teach him every day, not only are you teaching him how to process information, but you're also giving him the background knowledge he'll use in later years when faced with new situations.

A Tip from Sarahlynne

Helping Your Toddler to Become Metacognitive

- **Meet your little one where he is in his progress.** Let him be independent when he can handle it and help him when he feels frustrated. For example, physically help him put the puzzle piece in the first time, and only verbally guide him the second time if he seems ready for that step.
- **Model an example of what you'd like to see.** Show and then tell him what you want him to do: "Turn around the puzzle piece and put it here." Guide his hand to the correct position.
- **Ask questions.** When he says something is broken or asks for help solving a problem (for example, his truck is stuck on the racetrack), ask, "What are you going to do, problem solver?" Give him some time to react, and if he doesn't, model the sentence, "I have an idea!" and verbalize your solution. Eventually, he will answer your question with, "I have an idea!" and solve the challenge himself. When he does this, praise and celebrate this independence.
- **Teach him to handle his frustration.** Help him keep his patience by talking through the problem, taking a break, or helping him. You can say, "It's okay! Try again!" and help him use one of the strategies mentioned above. Model this behavior yourself at any time of the day when you feel frustrated or impatient.
- **Anticipate growth.** Understand that your child may not complete the task perfectly for some time, and be okay with that.

Emotional Needs of Infants and Toddlers

From the beginning, a baby has emotions. He has no idea how to label them, what to do with them, or how to handle them, but he feels them. Can you imagine the joy and security your baby feels when he's cuddled and kissed? Or how frustrating it has to be when he's upset? He can't move, he can't go get the person he needs, and he can't even explain what he wants. All he can do is cry louder and louder, with more desperation, hoping someone will hear him. The good news is that an infant's needs are elementary. Food, diaper change, feeling comfort, and receiving love and attention are his top requests. He doesn't have more complex emotional needs until later. But it's important to recognize that even basic emotional needs are just as important as physical ones.

Basic emotional needs

An infant is too young to "manipulate" his caregiver. He's trying to replicate the safety he had in the womb, and when he cries for you, he needs attention and security. Just as you wouldn't deny him food or a diaper change, denying his emotional connections is depriving him of a need. Penelope Leach, a well-known British psychologist, states, "Without food or warmth he will die; without social attention from adults he will not learn to live as a full human being." Dr. Leach gives an example of a mother who waits until a predetermined feeding time to feed her child. The baby is so worked up and upset by the time the mother goes to feed him that he does not greet his mother with a smile, cannot settle down to eat, and may not even eat as much because he's so worked up from crying.

Leaving an infant to cry when he needs his caregiver actually makes the baby more anxious and demanding. He realizes that his needs will not be met right away, so he becomes nervous when he's alone because he doesn't trust that his caregiver will return. A baby does not learn anything positive when his needs are not met. In the first half of the first year, he cannot be "spoiled." Instead, if his needs aren't met, he learns that he is helpless and unimportant, and his confidence in his caregivers decreases. He now has a higher level of cortisol (the stress hormone), and because his limbic system is working overtime to handle the excess cortisol, his frontal lobe (area of the brain that controls problem solving and cognitive function) can slow in development. We will discuss this process in more detail in Chapter 2.

What NOW?

Books to Help You Understand Your Baby's Temperament

- *The Happiest Baby on the Block* by Harvey Karp, M.D.
- *Temperament Tools: Working with Your Child's Inborn Traits* by Helen Neville, Diane Clark Johnson, and Dave Garbot
- *Your Baby and Child* by Penelope Leach

Babies are all different and will respond to different comforting tactics. For example, some will be happy to snuggle, and others will respond to swaddling or rocking. The key is to use those first few weeks to learn which response helps your baby to relax. High-needs babies will test the patience of their caregivers, but it's important that the caregiver try to console the baby whenever possible, even if that means taking a break and giving the baby to another caregiver for a few minutes.

What do babies absolutely need from their caregivers?

Respect: A child will respond directly to the respect that parents and other caregivers build early in the relationship. As child development researcher Jenn Berman put it, "Having her feelings understood and normalized frees a child to move forward developmentally so she can concentrate on other tasks. It is comforting for her to know what she is feeling is a normal part of the human experience." Your baby needs to know that his feelings matter and that he's being respected for how he feels, even if he can't get what he wants.

Have you ever seen an infant or toddler being changed when he doesn't want to be? It's incredibly difficult for the parent. He'll kick, turn over, scream, or push the parent's hands away in annoyance. Some parents choose to ignore his protests and take the "I'm-the-boss" attitude. Other parents stop the diaper change in fear of their child's anger and attempt it again in a few minutes. Neither reaction is fully respecting the child.

Respecting your child doesn't mean ignoring his feelings, nor does it mean allowing him to get his way all the time. It *does* mean acknowledging your child's feelings, reflecting back, and changing the situation, if appropriate. For example, your nine-month-old is on his back, kicking his legs in protest of the diaper change. You say, "I know you want to play right now. You don't want to get your diaper changed. Right? This is going to be really fast, and then we're going to play! Lie still so we can do this quickly." Then the caregiver can place her hand on the child's stomach to show him what she means.

Reflecting back on your infant's feelings is a great strategy as he grows toward toddlerhood. Once his frustrations are recognized, he may have an easier time calming down and going along with your request. This tactic can even be used when you're trying to explain rules and boundaries to your child. Toddlers are notorious for pushing the limits and testing their parents. But if you remind him of the rules while respecting his frustration, he will eventually be more respecting of the boundaries that you set. For example, when we put away our holiday train after Christmas, my son, at two and a half, helped graciously, but then, when he realized the train was really going away, stomped his feet and yelled, "No!" in protest. I responded with, "You're angry that the train has to go away. Do you want to play with it?"

He stopped jumping up and down and yelled, "Play with train!"

I repeated my validation of his feelings. "You want to play with the train. You're so sad that we have to put the train away."

At this point, he was no longer using his body to communicate, just his words. In a calmer voice, he said, "Play with train."

I said, "I know you want to play with the train. I do too. But we have to put it away now. We'll take it out again another time. Let's play with some of the new toys that don't have to be put away, like your new pirate ship!"

He did calm down for the moment, but then days later reenacted the situation, stomping his feet and explaining to me that the train had to go away and that he had said, "No!" He didn't get upset again, however. He just wanted to talk through the situation. Weeks later, he still talked about the train, but in a nostalgic way, as in, "Train under tree. Train stopped!" as he remembered how the train had gotten stuck on its tracks while he played with it.

Sometimes your child won't respond well to this strategy. He may still throw himself on the floor in protest, kicking and shouting, even though you validated his feelings. But at least he'll know why you're removing him from a situation, and hopefully the next time will be easier or the tantrum will be shorter. Remember, it is extremely important that you, as the parent, set consistent boundaries but still acknowledge and respect your child's feelings. This way he'll feel safe, nurtured, and respected in his home environment.

Consistency: A young child needs a consistent caregiver to feel in control, safe, and loved. The children who struggle the most with behavior and emotional control are the ones who are bounced around from caregiver to caregiver, daycare to daycare, and who don't have any routine or predictability in their life. In the words of Dr. Leach, "Above all, he needs at least one of you to be his special person (because everything else follows from it), to talk to him and to love him so that he too learns to be a special individual person who can talk and who can love." Your child needs to know that his unique traits are loved and attended to by his caregiver; that his needs, both physical and emotional, are worth attention. So, whether you are home with your child or you have outside child care, be sure to choose one path and stay consistent. If he has a loving caregiver, he will feel happy and secure, whether that is at home with you, with a grandparent or a nanny, or at a child care facility.

Infants and toddlers thrive on consistency in their routine. They can't communicate well, but they find comfort and control in knowing the order of the day. For example, my son always takes a nap about 30 minutes after lunch. We've established this routine since infancy, and at two and a half, he's very aware of when his nap begins. In fact, some days he even goes upstairs by himself! Although sometimes this routine changes, most of the time his life is very predictable. Consequently, there aren't many arguments about what is coming next in his day. Alternatively, if a young child's routine constantly changes, he doesn't know what to expect from the situation. Therefore, he feels a higher level of stress and anxiety than necessary. Again, his stress hormone (cortisol) is increased, and his limbic system might suffer from being too stressed. He may also cry, act out, or misbehave because he feels out of control and nervous. Alternatively, if he has a consistent schedule, he can predict what's coming next, so he doesn't have to worry. His previous experiences (his background schema) with this routine comfort him.

As your child grows, he'll start to copy everything you do. Consistency in your reactions, but also in your behaviors, is extremely important at this stage. Your child is learning what to do and what not to do by watching you. My son is in that stage right now, especially with his dad. Everything my husband does my son wants to do, and this is not always a positive thing. One day last summer, my husband jumped off the side of the pool backward, and guess what? Two seconds later my son was standing on the edge of the pool, turned around, thinking he was going to jump in backward. I put my hands on his legs and said, "Turn around. We jump into the pool this way." I pointed toward the water. "You need to see the water so you don't hit your head."

My son looked at my husband, who quickly repeated what I said, and then jumped in, facing forward. Now that my son had heard it from both of us and seen my husband jump in correctly, he followed our direction and jumped in forward where I was waiting for him.

Watching your child emulate you is adorable. The first time he says "thank you" or gives you a kiss, you will absolutely melt! However, the imitation can also be terrifying. Are you the type of person who yells at other drivers on the road? Do you lose your temper and yell? Throw things? Don't be surprised if your child reacts the same way you do when he has those same feelings. One of the hardest parts of parenting is watching your child act out the behaviors you don't like in yourself. But it'll teach you to temper your reactions when things don't go your way. And it'll pay off when you see your child calmly react the way you have when he's angry, sad, or frustrated.

What Does Quality Time Really Mean?

Parenting theorists agree that giving our children quality time every day is key to their social, cognitive, and intellectual development. This is possible for all parents, even if you have only an hour with your child each day. You just have to focus on your child. It's easy for us to think we're giving our children our time. We're in the same room, after all. Our two children are playing happily on their own, or even if they're playing independently, we can see them, so this must count as quality time, right? I know I'm guilty of this. I'm cooking dinner while my son is playing, and my daughter is happily swinging in her baby swing, so that's quality time, right? Nope.

Giving your full attention

Parenting theorists suggest a minimum of one to three sessions a day of at least 20 minutes each where the parent gets down on the floor and interacts, giving her child complete attention and participating in activities the child enjoys. If you have more than one child, have your children take turns choosing the first and second play activity if they can't agree on what they'd like to play. Attentive playtime is just as useful for infants as it is for toddlers, so you can start early.

These interactions teach compassion, patience, leadership skills, and self-confidence (see Chapter 6). When you give your child your full attention, you're showing him that his type of play is meaningful, even if it seems boring to you. (And some days it will be so tedious to get on the floor and put a train through a tunnel . . . again.) Your child will love your attention and may want to play for hours. The time limits are just suggestions. If it's hard for you to sit and just play, start with 20 minutes per day, and add more time when you can.

The good news is that the emphasis is not on the quantity of time spent with your child. While some parents choose to stay home with their children, others do not or cannot. So they wonder, "Am I spending enough time with my children?" The answer is that all parents can make enough time for their children, even if they work outside the home. If you make your children your focus during certain times during the day—getting on the floor or being open for conversation, sharing, and questions—you are! It's about consistency, care, and quality time. Don't worry if you're not available every minute. Just be available when you can.

If you're not giving your child enough personal attention, he'll let you know. An infant may want to nurse more often during the night, because he's making up for lost time during the day. A toddler may have more meltdowns and tantrums because he feels like he's constantly fighting for your attention. You'll know your child's signals, and you'll know when he's satisfied. All children need a different amount of attention to fill their love cup, and only you will know when your child is content.

Resisting distraction, especially technology

When you're not playing with your child, he's still watching you. He sees everything. He's fascinated by you, your reactions, and what you do with your time. Children see our everyday activities as things they want to imitate, as natural parts of the world around them. So, if you vacuum every day, your child will try to pick up the vacuum cleaner too. If you're on your phone a lot, you'll see your toddler imitate that. And, if you use technology often, he sees your cell phone or computer as something he wants to use as often as you do.

If you don't want your child to rely on technology for entertainment, use your devices sparingly when he's awake. Zero to three is not the age to focus on showing your child how to entertain himself with electronic gadgets. He'll have plenty of opportunities to develop these skills as he gets older. Instead, use these years to introduce him to the multisensory details the world itself has to offer. With technology so prevalent in our daily lives, this is very easy for parents to forget. For example, I was out on a walk one day with my son. I pulled out my phone and checked my email. I chose that moment because he seemed completely enthralled by jumping in puddles. But then he looked up at me to share in the joy of the puddle-jumping, and I was looking down at my little plastic distraction. So what did I teach him in that minute? That being outside and playing in puddles isn't enough? That I need more stimulation than the fun that comes with being outside? Not my finest moment.

Of course, there is a time and a place for technology. If we use it carefully, it can be useful and helpful. Ever been on an airplane with a toddler? Books downloaded on an iPad® can be a peacemaker!

How Your Relationship with Your Child Fits In

Parenting is an extremely detailed job. While it's about the big picture, it's also about the hundreds of choices you make each day. The choices are where the patterns are created. If your pattern as a parent is to devote about 20 minutes of quality time to your child a few times a day (this doesn't include the time that you are casually hanging out with your child while you complete other household tasks), your toddler (especially) will be more likely to let you attend to your needs, because he knows that the pattern is that you will soon come back and play again. For example, if you always play for 20 minutes before you cook dinner, your toddler will come to recognize that as the pattern and will eventually learn that after your playtime with him he has to play by himself for the 30 minutes or so it takes for you to put a meal on the table. So during this focused play, it's important to be fully present and engaged, so he knows this is his time.

Don't stress if you can't be with your children all the time. It's not only okay, but also good for their development to learn patience and independence and rely on that background schema of knowing that you will return. These skills will serve him well in unchartered situations, and you will feel much better as a parent knowing that you don't have to entertain your child all the time for him to be content.

This book will help make you aware of what you're doing when you're around your baby, what you're saying, and how you're spending your time with him. As you read, keep in mind that all the domains of development are intricately interrelated. All of the chapters are connected. The relationships, experiences, and environments that surround your infant and toddler will be key to his sensory, motor, physical, language, and emotional development. Often, the same techniques you use to promote language development will be the ones you look to for emotional growth. Each piece of your child's growth is built upon his previous experience, which in turn create his background schema and cognitive, physical, and emotional development.

However, it's also important to understand that all children develop differently and at their own pace. This can be incredibly difficult if all of your child's friends are walking but your child is still crawling. Or maybe all your child's friends can count to 10 and he still can't. Be confident that your child will get there, and know that child development will come in bursts. One day your child will suddenly be running with ease, even though yesterday he may have been awkwardly moving in a walking-and-running combination. And then he'll pause in his other skills for a bit, as he practices and learns the appropriate context for this new skill. He may even regress in other skills as he focuses on this new, exciting ability. (Ever seen a baby who's just learned to stand up? He'll do it all night long, just because he can! Forget about sleep for a while.) He'll amaze you, and he'll do it at his own pace.

These years are critical. Your baby's cognitive and emotional functions are developing at a rapid pace, and your decisions and reactions to him are setting the stage for how he will grow and change over the next few years. Now that we've covered what's happening in his brain and how his emotional centers are developing, in the next chapter we're going to talk more about the countless benefits of the bonding process and how connecting with your child can encourage strong cognitive and emotional development.

Notes:

Chapter Preview

- How to bond with your infant or toddler
- What to do if you don't feel an emotional connection to your baby
- How to respond to your baby's cues
- The power of routine
- Bonding activities for you and your baby

Chapter 2

Connecting and Bonding with Your Baby

What does it mean to bond with your baby? Most of the time, we bond with our children without thinking about it. We interact with them, respond, and try to keep their stress levels low. For example, when you take your infant to a social gathering, maybe you keep her in her car seat for the first few minutes so that she gets used to the scenery. Then, you take her out and cradle her, put her in a sling, or sit her up so that she can see her environment. If she's comfortable, you may allow others to hold and snuggle her as well. This type of stimulation and bonding can boost cognitive and emotional development. Your baby knows that she's part of the socialization activity, so she feels safe, included, and loved.

You may do this naturally for your baby's comfort, but actually you are fulfilling your baby's essential needs. She needs and craves attention to grow. Those who say that a baby can or should be left alone when she cries because "she only wants attention" do not understand that her need for socialization and attention is just as important as her need for food.

Building Trust

Much of the recent research argues that newborns and infants need unlimited snuggles, feeding on demand, and as many bonding opportunities as possible in order to feel safe enough to grow and learn. Therefore, schedules should not be the focus right away.

One of the most important approaches you can take with your newborn is to respond promptly to her needs. Your response reduces her stress and allows her social development to occur appropriately. Dr. Penelope Leach asserts that by not responding, you're teaching your baby that you won't tend to her when she needs you, listen when she's unhappy, or give her what she wants when she asks. So, in turn, the baby learns that her voice has no merit, her self-confidence is low, and she will be unhappy to be alone or play alone because she will associate the experience with loneliness and despair.

But at times your baby will have to wait while you get your older child a glass of milk or finish a toileting session with your toilet-learning toddler. You won't always get to your baby the second she starts fussing, and you won't always know what's wrong. That's okay. Your constant efforts matter. Your baby trusts that she's safe and loved, so she can tackle everything else. She is constantly inundated with new stimuli every time she opens her eyes, but she finds comfort, predictability, and safety from the attention and nurturing that her primary caregiver provides. In Chapter 1, we talked about brain development. A baby cannot absorb all the new stimuli she's facing if she doesn't feel safe in her environment. And that's what a strong and trusting relationship with a caregiver will give a young child: the ability to relax enough to learn.

Comforting your infant during the fourth trimester

Pediatrician Harvey Karp argues that during the first three months of an infant's life, parents need to replicate as much of the womb as possible to make their baby feel safe, stimulated, and nurtured. When we try to quiet our baby's environment in early life, we're actually creating more stress. Dr. Karp's well-known theory of the "fourth trimester" states that babies who are placed in perfectly quiet rooms are under-stimulated, and that's why they cry. All the jostling and warmth of the womb actually makes it a noisy place. For example, for the first two weeks of my daughter's life, we noticed that that she slept much better at night if we left the television on. During the day, she napped especially well when I had the dishwasher, electric mixer, or laundry on within her earshot. However, by the time she was about six weeks old, she was completely comfortable sleeping without noise at night. During the day, though, she still did very well sleeping in the family room while everyone was playing and talking!

There are other ways to keep your baby comfortable during the fourth trimester. Dr. Karp suggests swaddling (to replicate the coziness of the womb), white noise while sleeping, "shushing," constant touch or baby-wearing, and breast-feeding on demand or allowing your baby to have a pacifier. These techniques will lessen your baby's stress because instead of quickly pushing her out of her old world, you are gently easing her into her new one.

What if you don't bond with your baby right away?

When we're preparing to parent a child, we're bombarded with comments about how awesome it's going to feel to have one. We're told how sweet babies are, how much we're going to love them, and how wonderful our new life will be. But what if you have your baby and this doesn't happen? What if you secretly feel guilty because you didn't fall in love with your baby immediately? What if you miss your old life more than you thought?

It's okay. This is actually a common occurrence that just isn't discussed enough. We don't always instantly bond with our children, just as we don't naturally bond with everyone we meet. So don't worry if you didn't get that "magical moment" as soon as you held your child. Some moms get nervous if they aren't able to bond with their baby right away. Maybe the baby needed some extra care from the doctors and couldn't be with mom right away. Perhaps the mom is struggling with postpartum blues or is not breast-feeding. Or maybe the mom adopted her baby several weeks or months after the birth. Any one of these moms might be worried that she and her baby won't have a special bond because the "window" has been missed.

While these initial bonding moments are wonderful and important, they do not define bonding. Connecting to your child is a long process; it's a journey, not a onetime event. The key is to be there consistently for your baby so that your baby can depend on your love, care, and attention. It's one thing to *make* a child, but it's a totally different thing to *parent* one. You have countless opportunities to create a long-lasting, trusting relationship with your baby. Many new parents (even second- or third-time parents!) feel overwhelmed when their baby arrives. Physical recovery, exhaustion, new responsibilities, and a messy house can contribute to temporary feelings of anxiety, sadness, or frustration. It's a common feeling, and some new parents feel better after a few weeks.

However, 10% of moms who give birth will feel more severe symptoms of postpartum blues. This is called *postpartum depression*, and some adoptive parents experience a syndrome called *post-adoptive depression*. Postpartum depression can include irritability, a loss of appetite, trouble sleeping, high anxiety, depression, or thoughts of hurting yourself or your child. If you feel these symptoms, and they seem to only get worse and last for weeks, it's time to see your doctor, says Dr. Neill Epperson, of the Yale University School of Medicine. Remember that your doctor and other trained professionals are there to help you, and it's okay to ask for help and assistance.

Responding to Your Infant

Newborns cry when they're feeling stressed and out of control. Isn't that why all of us cry? And just as we enjoy and thrive on support and love when we feel upset and sad, so does a baby. Of course, some people will tell you that it's wrong to pick up a crying infant, that you are "spoiling her" by giving too much attention. To lots of recent parenting researchers, that's ludicrous. If our spouse or friend is upset, we offer comfort. We don't ask them to wait 10 minutes until they've "self-soothed." We immediately go to them with a hug or sit with them while they tell us their frustrations. We listen and we support.

Infants need this same love and tenderness, but actually for more important reasons. According to pediatrician T. Berry Brazelton and child psychiatrist Stanley Greenspan, "Family patterns that undermine nurturing care may lead to significant compromise in both cognitive and emotional capacities." On the other hand, "Supportive, warm, nurturing emotional interactions with infants and young children help the nervous system grow appropriately." Dr. Jenn Berman argues that "a child whose cries are consistently responded to in a negative way—he is yelled at, for example, or abused or neglected—is likely to become anxious in anticipation of a negative reaction from his parents." Each time a child is in need, she begins to expect that she'll have to fight for her parent's attention, so her stress hormone levels increase, and her brain can become wired for anxiety issues later on.

Scientifically, it works like this. Your baby is crying because she's hungry or wants attention. The parents "wait" a predetermined amount of time before responding. The adrenal glands in the baby then release cortisol. Too much released cortisol "floods" the brain and can "destroy nerve connections in critical portions of an infant's developing brain," says attachment parenting specialist William Sears, M.D. Long-term effects can include attention-deficit hyperactivity disorder (ADHD), higher anxiety, aggression, and impulsiveness. Conversely, researchers explain, "Sensitive, responsive, secure caretaking plays an important role in buffering or blocking elevations in cortisol for infants and young children." If less cortisol is released, the developing brain can continue to function normally.

Furthermore, the baby learns by experience how she deserves to be treated. If her parent soothes and cares for her when she's upset or frustrated, she comes to expect that she should be treated with respect, setting the stage for higher self-esteem later on. A baby who is responded to and cared for with respect will have less anxiety, better social skills, and regulate her emotions better as she grows.

How your infant communicates with you

In order to respond and keep your baby's stress level low, you have to know what you're looking for. The trick is to recognize her signals. (Hint: Crying is her last resort!)

One of the ways a newborn will communicate stress is through her *Moro reflex*, sometimes called the "startle reflex." An infant performs this action when she's been put down carelessly or without enough attention. When an infant's Moro reflex activates, her arms jerk and reach toward yours, and her legs will reach upward, searching for a body to hold onto. She's instinctively trying to protect herself and trying to hold onto something so she will not be dropped. She doesn't know that she's being set down on a soft surface, so her protective instincts take over. When she reacts this way, it's because she is startled and stressed. So if you see your baby's Moro reflex, take notice, and the next time you're putting her down, hold her back and head for a few more seconds as you gently lay her down.

The Moro reflex, sometimes called the "startle reflex," is one way that a newborn communicates stress.

When you pick her up, try to avoid just scooping her up into your arms without warning. That startles her! Instead, gently stroke her arms or tummy and announce your arrival, with a soft, "Hi, cutie! Come with me!" before you reach down to move her to a new location. This will help ease the transition, lessening her stress level because the movement isn't a surprise.

A newborn also knows how to communicate "I'm hungry!" without crying. When she's ready to nurse or take a bottle, she'll use her *rooting reflex*. She'll purse her lips, as if she's about to kiss, as she "roots" for a nipple or bottle. She may also lick her lips or put her hands in her mouth, expressing a desire to eat. If you see her performing one of these behaviors, offer milk and you will lower her stress level and teach her how to communicate without tears. Crying is her last attempt at getting fed; it is her distress call to you.

If your baby is extremely stressed, she will, of course, cry, but you may also see her startle, excessively cry, shake, or arch her back. These are all signs that need to be taken seriously, and you should avoid putting your baby in situations that would warrant this kind of reaction.

An infant who wants to play will look at you, smile, or reach for a toy. However, when she's tired, she may turn her head to look away from the stimulation, or even get the hiccups! By the way, did you know that hiccups in newborns could represent overstimulation?

Pay close attention to your baby's cues, and after a few months, you'll know exactly how she reacts when she wants or needs something from her caregivers.

How to respond to your baby's cues

Even if you understand most of your baby's needs, there will still be times when she cries. Maybe you didn't get to her fast enough, or maybe your efforts to soothe were not what she wanted. You can't prevent your infant from ever crying, but you can respond as soon as possible when she is crying. And actually, studies have shown that "increased responsiveness to fussing or crying infants lessens the overall amount of infant crying."

Soothing: You've already helped by going quickly to your crying baby. Picking her up, rocking her, baby-wearing, nursing her, saying "shh" in a constant stream, or talking with her in a gentle tone are all appropriate soothing techniques. Even if she continues to cry, keep holding her.

Parents sometimes think that their efforts are futile and the baby "just wants to be left alone." Babies do not want to be left alone, but they can't always communicate what it is that they do want. Experiment with holding your baby in various positions to see which she responds to the best. I knew an infant who loved being held in what his father referred to as the "football hold." Dad would lay his son on his stomach and balance him on his forearm, bouncing him gently. His son was able to see everything and showed very low stress in this position. In contrast, my kids loved to be held so that they could rest their head on my shoulder or look around and see everything from a high vantage point.

Vibration and white noise are also key soothing techniques for some infants, especially colicky ones. One mother held her son in his baby seat on top of the clothes dryer, and its vibrations comforted him. Another mother carried her baby in a sling while she vacuumed, and the bouncing and sound of the vacuum cleaner soothed him. My kids loved the white noise of a hair drier. We'd put them in their baby seat in the bathroom while I dried my hair, and they would instantly calm down.

Here's a little trick: When soothing your crying baby, find a consistent sound or song that you sing each time she's feeling stressed. She'll eventually associate this sound with you and calmness, and will begin to relax even if she just hears it. This is a lifesaver if you have a baby who's screaming in her car seat while you're on the road. Choose a sound, like "shh," or an easy song with few lyrics, like "Twinkle, Twinkle, Little Star." My husband used this method inadvertently with our son, singing the song in the hospital while the nurses gave him his first bath, and it was so incredibly beneficial. It worked for almost 16 months and saved us many times from having to pull over to the side of the road for an emergency snuggle session!

When you're with your child and you respond to her needs, you also learn her less obvious signals so that she'll cry less, have more of her needs met, and feel safer. Of course, you may not always be able to be with your child. Perhaps you work outside the home or are pulled away from your baby because of other obligations. When putting your child in someone else's hands, keep one thing in mind, say Drs. Brazelton and Greenspan: Keep the care consistent. As mentioned in Chapter 1, it's very unhealthy for a baby to be frequently shuffled from caregiver to caregiver. She will not create a strong bond with anyone and will feel anxious and stressed when you leave because of the lack of predictability in her schedule. Make every effort to choose the same attentive caregiver each time, so your child will feel safe and will trust that you will return.

Many parents work during the day or are away on trips so they don't have as much concentrated time with their child. However, if this parent sets aside time as often as possible for planned play or bonding time, the child will develop just as strong a bond with this parent as she has with her other caregiver.

The question of "cry-it-out": Research suggests that the so-called cry-it-out method is inappropriate, at least for newborns. Before six months, your baby just doesn't have the cognitive ability to know why you're leaving. Yes, the baby will fall asleep, but from sheer exhaustion, not from self-soothing. In Dr. Leach's words, "Leaving him to howl cannot be the right answer . . . he is not settling happily and being abandoned will certainly increase his feeling that it is not safe to let you go out of the room in case you never

What NOW?

Books with Sleeping Solutions

- *The Baby Sleep Book: The Complete Guide to a Good Night's Rest for the Whole Family* by William Sears, M.D.
- *The Happiest Baby Guide to Great Sleep: Simple Solutions for Kids from Birth to 5 Years* by Harvey Karp, M.D.
- *I Had My Baby! What Happens Now? A Pediatrician's Essential Guide to the First 6 Months* by Robert Lindeman, M.D.
- *The No-Cry Sleep Solution: Gentle Ways to Help Your Baby Sleep through the Night* by Elizabeth Pantley
- *Solve Your Child's Sleep Problems* by Richard Ferber, M.D.

come back." After your baby gets a little older, between five and seven months, she'll have the ability to understand that it's bedtime, and you may have to teach her how to fall asleep without rocking, nursing, or snuggling. So, at that point, you might choose to use the cry-it-out method, in which a baby is left for short times to learn to soothe herself. But do it sparingly, keep it controlled, and explain the process to your child. You do not want to break the trust and bond you've worked so hard to create.

Cry-it-out does not mean allowing your baby to cry for as long as it takes for her to fall asleep. Instead, this method advocates leaving the baby for short, controlled intervals. Dr. Richard Ferber, who developed the "Ferber method" popularly associated with this technique, recommends it only as a last resort.

If you're uncomfortable with the cry-it-out method, there are other techniques to use. Your baby's stress level will be lessened during a gentler process. See the sidebar for a list of books that address this subject.

Infants, Toddlers, and the Power of Routines

After you've moved past the newborn and infant stage, in which you have to play detective to figure out what's wrong, you think you're in the clear. And then comes . . . the toddler. The toddler who screams and throws temper tantrums and might show frustration by throwing, kicking, or even biting. You long for the days when a song and a snuggle would calm her, because now you have a child who knows what she wants and hates when she can't have it now.

However, if you've spent the first year responding to your infant, you'll naturally respond to your toddler, and you'll most likely have a much calmer, happier child.

You may not even have to deal with some of these negative behaviors on a regular basis. The basic rule here, just as it was when she was an infant, is respect. Listen and respond to her voice. For instance, if you're out shopping and it's naptime, and your child is not one to sleep in her stroller, she may begin to rub her eyes. Next, she may start crying or saying, "No! No!" trying to escape her stroller. Finally, she may start kicking, pulling objects off shelves, and making it abundantly clear that she needs to go home *now*. At this point, you may be incredibly frustrated with her behavior. But in fact, your toddler is actually right. It's naptime. She knows it. She wants to be home in her bed, and she tried to tell you, but you didn't hear her, so she had to tell you in a more dramatic fashion.

If it's time to go home, go home. If your child is respected and her routine is respected, she'll be much happier and less likely to have emotional meltdowns.

Creating a daily routine

Infants and toddlers respond incredibly well to routines. Schedules keep infants calm, but they do even more for toddlers. They give them a sense of control, belonging, trust, self-confidence, and independence. Well-respected routines tell a child, "You are important and your life is important." When your child is an infant, she'll fall into her own routine within the first few months. Soon, through your sleep-deprived state, you'll see that she wants to eat at about the same time each day and take a nap around the same time each day. Then, you'll start to get a bit of your life back; you can leave the house, knowing approximately when your child will need something. Some people might tell you that you can put your newborn on a schedule, but that allowing her to create the schedule is "spoiling her." Nope. Infants have no idea that there is a day or night time, but will learn these concepts slowly, over time. Allow your baby to set the schedule. Listen to her needs and respond to her cues. Allow her to eat when she needs to, sleep when she needs to, and snuggle when she wants to. If you do this when she's very small, you'll be creating a bond of trust and respect. After a few months, you'll most likely find that she has fallen into a schedule of play, eat, and sleep throughout the day. There's no need to rush it.

At six months or so, your baby's routine will be more consistent. And as she grows, routines will give your child control over her day, and she will be much less likely to become upset or frustrated. Certain events will be unexpected, but if they are sandwiched between routine events, there will be much less stress put upon your child. This doesn't mean that you should never deviate from your child's schedule. Actually, it's good to do so at times. You'll teach your child flexibility and the ability to handle new situations, all the while knowing that she'll have the predictability of her schedule when the new event is done.

In creating a daily routine, follow your baby's cues. If your baby occasionally falls asleep on your chest while you rest, that may be a good solution to naptime.

In fact, your child's routine will naturally change (usually just as you get used to the one routine you've just introduced!) as she gets older. For example, she'll move from three naps a day to two, to one, and finally to quiet playtime in the afternoon. She'll begin by nursing or bottle-feeding six to eight times a day, then she'll start solids in conjunction with her milk feedings, and eventually, she'll sit at the table and eat what has been cooked for the family when the family eats. Know that each phase is fleeting. Your job is to respond to your changing and growing child and adjust her routines when she shows the interest.

What does an infant's daily routine look like? An infant's daily routine can be quite predictable because it cycles through the same few activities all day. Exciting, I know. A typical sequence is as follows:

Wake up. Perhaps bottle-feeding or nursing.

Active time for quiet learning, play, and interaction. When your infant is quiet but also alert, she is primed for learning. Place an object in front of her and slowly move it from side to side. Smile at her and talk to her. Lay her down where she can see her reflection or shadow, or just allow her to stare at whatever she is looking at. She's absorbing it all and learning every minute.

Perhaps another feeding. Some babies like to nurse or have a bottle before sleeping, whereas others do not.

Nap. A good time for a walk or a drive! Infants have a sleep cycle of about 40 minutes. Your baby may wake up after 40 minutes or may sleep through another sleep cycle. Most infants nap every 60 to 90 minutes, but some do not do this on their own and have to be taught to nap. You can do this by reading your baby's sleepy signals (yawning, closing her eyes), calming her when she's tired by bouncing her on your shoulder or giving her some time in an infant swing, and placing her in her crib on a schedule.

Repeat until bedtime.

A toddler's daily routine: Toddler schedules can vary greatly, depending on your toddler's personality, your family's schedule, and your children's needs and desires. Here is a sample sequence:

Wake up.

Breakfast.

Play date, preschool, errands with parent, outdoor play. This period includes some type of active play. Sometimes the child may have a snack during this activity as well.

Lunch.

Individual play.

Nap.

Snack.

Indoor play, quiet time, or craft activity. This may be a great time for scheduled playtime with parent! See Chapter 6.

Shorter outdoor play, active play, play date.

Dinner.

Individual play.

Bath.

Bedtime routine.

Handling temper tantrums: It can be a joy to create a daily routine by responding to your baby's cues. But how do you maintain that routine during your toddler's temper tantrums? Although routines will prevent some tantrums, even the most organized parent will have a child who shows her displeasure by screaming, kicking, and throwing dramatic tantrums. Every child will try this behavior, but the parent's response to these emotional outbursts will teach the child if they are accepted or unaccepted behaviors. A tantrum is an incredibly intense moment for a toddler. She wants something and doesn't understand why she can't have it immediately. Your answers are ridiculous to her, and because she doesn't have the words or ability to verbally rationalize with you, she reacts the only way she knows how: through crying and screaming.

A tantrum can be extremely frustrating for a parent (especially if it's in a public place!), but it's so important for you to put yourself in your baby's shoes, try to stay calm, and respond in a respectful way. How you respond to your child's tantrums is, as one researcher said, "one of the greatest predictors of how he will turn out as a young man. It affects his ability to regularly empathize with people and thus maintain relationships—big factors in human happiness."

The key is to acknowledge your child's feelings, validate them, and then teach her to label the feeling she's experiencing, even if she can't get what she wants. Get down to her level so that she can see your face, calmly listen, and respond to her feelings. For example, if it's bedtime and your child doesn't want to brush her teeth, she may stomp and scream in protest. Remember to acknowledge, validate, and teach. Here is a suggested response:

> *Parent, kneeling to child's level:* You want to play now. You don't want to brush your teeth.
>
> *Child:* Play!
>
> *Parent:* I know you want to play. I do too! You're angry because we have to brush your teeth. So let's brush your teeth quickly and then we'll play again.
>
> *Child:* No teeth! Play with toys!
>
> *Parent:* You want to play with toys? Okay. Let's brush our teeth and then play with toys.
>
> *Child:* Why? Play with toys!
>
> *Parent:* [Repeats the same sentiment as above, a few more times if necessary.]

If your child then follows you into the bathroom, that's great. If not, lead her to the bathroom and follow through with your promise. Quickly brush her teeth and then give her a few minutes to play. This strategy may not stop the tantrum immediately, but your child will eventually learn that she doesn't need to act in such a dramatic way because her feelings are heard and respected.

Alternatively, responding with silliness can "surprise" your toddler out of a temper tantrum. Acting incredibly ridiculous, such as getting on the floor and acting like your child's favorite animal, or speaking in a hysterical, overdramatic voice may distract your child enough for her to relax and calm down.

Bonding at bedtime

Bedtime routines for infants can be simple: bath, pajamas, snuggles, nursing or bottle-feeding, and bed. Your baby will come to expect and enjoy it, and will relax during this time, knowing it's just you and her with no other distractions. Bedtime is a beautiful time for cozy bonding.

With a toddler, you may get a bit more creative. Just be sure to set limits or your toddler may want to read stories for an hour! For example, you may establish a sequence of tooth-brushing, bath, pajamas, three books, two songs, snuggles, and bed. Be prepared for your child to add to the routine. My son went through a phase in which he needed to sleep with his toy bus and airplane, and they had to be in the crib before we could say good night. He played until he tired, and then we heard a loud "thud!" as he threw them out of the crib. When we'd go back up to his room a few minutes later, he'd be snuggled in his crib, sleeping. A few months later, when we transitioned him to a bed, he decided that he wanted to cuddle cheek to cheek with us a few times before hugs and kisses. He called this "cheeks!" and insisted upon it each night.

These additions to my son's bedtime routine gave him a little control and made him feel important and heard. Toddlers may feel that they have almost zero control over anything in their lives, so it's important to provide some opportunities in which they can have a say over a part of the day.

Bedtime routines are also essential for parent–child bonding, especially for the parent who is away all day. Spend the time allowing your child to choose her stories, and read them slowly and with enthusiasm, allowing her to point out the pictures or snuggle with you if she prefers. In fact, if one parent is home all day and the other works outside the home, it can be a wonderful idea to have this working parent put the child to bed. That way this parent can have her daily time with her child that is just for the two of them.

If you're a stay-at-home parent, and you just started hyperventilating a little, don't worry. I get it. Allowing the more absent parent to step in and "take over" can sometimes be hard for the one who is with the child all day. In my case, I am home all day with my children, and so it was at first hard to "trust" that my husband would do all the "right" things. He does things differently. And it's okay. But it took me months to come to that conclusion. Your child will respond differently to her other parent, learn new things, and be given new challenges. As uncomfortable as this can be for the parent who is with the child more often, it's really important to trust your partner, step back, and see what happens. You might be pleasantly surprised.

Sometimes your child will have difficulty settling down and going to sleep. She may be going through a separation anxiety phase, or she may just not want to be alone to go to sleep. Experts suggest a "patience" technique that is useful for older infants and young toddlers who are not practiced at self-soothing. During the day, help your child learn patience by explaining that she's going to wait for certain objects, such as a snack

A Tip from Sarahlynne

Bedtime Tricks and Techniques

- **Start with soft toys.** Give your child a stuffed animal to snuggle with, a pacifier, or a few toys to play with as she becomes sleepy.
- **Use soothing sounds.** A sound machine or soft music can lull her into calmness.
- **Respond to your baby as soon as she's tired.** An overstimulated baby is harder to put to sleep. Watch for signs of sleepiness, such yawning or rubbing her eyes.
- **Make the routine cozy, consistent, and relaxing.** For example, read a story, sing a song, turn off the overhead lights and switch on the nightlight, and then make a big deal out of all of her stuffed animals saying good night to her and either staying in the crib or jumping out.
- **Describe the routine.** When she gets old enough, ask her to verbalize each step of the bedtime routine every night so that she feels in control and can predict each step.
- **Give her some say over her bedtime routine.** Invite her to choose the stories, or ask her to decide which pajamas to wear.
- **Place a chair next to her crib.** Sit on that chair the first night, say good night, and wait for her to fall asleep. Every night, move the chair farther away, until you are sitting outside the door. (This strategy works best with a toddler who understands what you're doing.)

or a toy. Start small, by having her wait 15 to 20 seconds, and add time until you get to a minute. Name an action rather than a time span, since your child will have not yet learned the meaning of time. For example, if your toddler asks for a snack, you can say, "I'm going to finish folding this laundry, and then I'll get you your snack." After doing this for about a week, try the next step at bedtime. Put her to bed normally, but in the middle of your routine, exclaim, "Oh, I forgot to put the dishes away! Be right back!" Run out of the room, and come back 15 to 20 seconds later. She'll be used to waiting at this point, so it shouldn't be too difficult for her. If she protests your leaving, instead complete a quick "chore" in her room. The next night, stay out of the room a bit longer, and the next night, a bit longer. Eventually, while she waits, she may just fall asleep!

Bonding Activities for You and Your Baby

Bonding with your child not only meets her emotional and physical needs but also allows her curiosity, imagination, and cognitive functions to properly and optimally develop. Even the caregiver who isn't always present can bond with his child using activities in the time that is available.

Activities for Ages 0–1

- Infant massage. Massage is a wonderful way to relax your baby and can even be performed on healthy newborns. It has been shown to have medical benefits, such as reducing colic, constipation, and gas, as well as strengthening the digestive and respiratory systems. Teresa Kirkpatrick Ramsey, BSN, LMT, adds, "Stimulating the nervous system through the skin may help build muscle tone, coordination, and brain functioning." Follow the guidelines of Ramsey and Dr. Jenn Berman for a great massage session with your infant:
  - Check with your child's pediatrician first.
  - Don't massage a baby who has a fever.
  - Tell your baby about the massage before you begin.
  - Use baby oil if your child's skin can tolerate it.
  - Remove all hand and wrist jewelry.
  - Wait an hour after baby eats.
  - Keep the room warm, or keep your baby clothed.

(continued)

- If your baby fusses, turns red, closes her eyes, turns away, tenses, or gets the hiccups, she is overstimulated. Stop the massage and try another time.
- Massage her legs first; it is a less intimate spot. Support her left ankle with one hand and with the other hand smoothly stroke her leg from ankle to hip.
- Place your baby on her back and put your palms in the center of her chest. Move your hands outward, toward her sides. Move your hands down and around and back to the center of her chest, like an upside-down heart.
- Place her on her tummy (if she wants), and place your hand horizontally below her neck. Move your hand down toward her bottom. Lift your hand at the bottom of her back, and follow with the next hand. Repeat.
- Repeat a movement several times in one spot. Using gentle pressure, glide the tips of your fingers on your baby's skin, but don't pull.

- Face time. Your infant will love looking in your eyes and studying your face. She's trying to figure out emotional cues, and she can do this by studying the changes in your face. Show her various expressions, such as "happy," "surprised," "excited," and "sad." She should play this game with any of her long-term caregivers so that she learns to interpret the differences in each person's expressions.
- **Laughter.** Make silly faces at her, kiss her, or sing a silly song. By the way, there is no one who can make a baby laugh more than an older sibling!
- **Photo album.** Show pictures of family members and close friends. Tell your baby who each person is while pointing to their faces.
- **Plush greeting.** If your baby wakes up quietly from the night's sleep or a nap before you get her out of her crib, hold a stuffed animal between the bars of the crib and crouch down beside the crib (hide if you think this will add to the drama). Make the toy dance and say, "Time to get up!" Then pop up and say, "Good morning" with a smile and a hug. This ritual can provide a pleasant start to your morning routine! (Eric and Geeta L., parents of two)
- **Bath time.** Sit in the bath together and play with bath toys like ducks, fish, and cups.

Activities for Ages 1–3

- **"Catch you!" game.** Play a version of "going to get you!" that your baby is comfortable with. If you child likes to hide behind you, ask, "Where is ______?" Wait for the giggles and turn around and laugh, saying, "There you are!" This is a great activity for when you're waiting in line at the grocery store and your child is in the cart. "Pretend" you can't find her and look up and down until she makes a sound. When she gets a little older, she may even say, "I'm right here!" Some crawling babies will find it hilarious if you crawl with them, saying, "I'm going to get you!" in a *playful voice. Crawl toward your baby slowly, allowing her to get away a bit, and then make a big dramatic move toward her. When you do choose to "catch" her, use kisses and soft touch. (Refrain from tickling. See Chapter 3.)*

- **Cocoon game.** Lie in a blanket or sleeping bag, and have your toddler do the same. Stay quiet, hold hands and touch, and then, after a while, pretend you have become butterflies and fly out of your cocoon.
- **Bag of tricks.** Fill a bag full of miniature household items (toy vacuum, wagon, coffee cup, stroller) and invite your child to take out one at a time. Have him tell you how to use that item and talk about how he's seen you use it in the house. (Mary G., mother of two)
- **Postcards.** Buy a postcard that shows your city. Have your toddler decorate the back with stickers. Send it to a grandparent or an aunt or uncle.
- **Ramp and ball.** Create a ramp with an ironing board and a low table or a few pillows. Keep the board safely secured. Have your toddler sit or stand at the bottom of the ramp and you stand at the top. Roll a ball down the ramp and have your child catch it. Change positions after a few minutes, or raise the ramp slightly higher.
- **Human basketball hoop.** Open your arms into the shape of a hoop. Give your child a plush ball and have her throw the ball into your "handmade hoop."
- **Little fort.** Use pillows and a blanket or a box to make a tunnel. Climb into the fort with your toddler, bring some toys inside, and have a special place just for the two of you to play in.
- **Animal sounds and movements.** Have your toddler be the leader. Copy her, and do the movements next to her. For example, she could hop like a frog or gallop like a horse.
- **Fun walking and running.** Lead your toddler (or let her lead you!) in creative strides. For example, march with your knees high, walk on your tiptoes swing your arms wide, or crouch down low while walking.
- **Traditional activities.** Play the games you played as a child, such as "Red light, green light" or "What time is it, Mr. Fox?" Or just bring out the jump rope or hula hoop.
- **Mirror play.** Pick up your toddler so that she can see in a mirror. Playfully ask, "Who do you see in the mirror?" Give absurd choices like Elmo, Cookie Monster, or her best friend. Then, say, "It's [your child's name]!"

Chapter Preview

- How to gently expand your baby's world
- The development of a baby's physical and motor skills
- The sensory experiences of infants and toddlers
- Physical, motor, and sensory activities for your baby

Chapter 3

Your Baby's Physical, Motor, and Sensory Experiences

How does your baby first see the world? During the first few months of life, a baby's vision is still developing. A newborn can easily focus only on objects that are within 8 to 10 inches of his face. He recognizes his mother's voice, having heard it for hours each day while in the womb, and possibly her partner's, if he's heard that voice often during the pregnancy. His mother's voice comforts him more than anything; her touch calms him. He thrives on soft touch and on studying faces.

You may find your infant gazing into your eyes. He's taking what's comforting to him (your voice and touch) and reconciling it with how you look. He isn't yet aware that he himself has eyes, a nose, and a mouth (this will come later, and it's so adorable!), but for now, he's in awe of every detail of your face. He'll soon connect your face with food and comfort. As Drs. Brazelton and Greenspan point out, "An infant studies her parents' faces, cooing and returning their smiles with a special glow of her own as they woo each other and learn about love together."

Your baby is all about you. This bonding time is so beautiful and poignant and sets the groundwork for the physical, motor, and sensory experiences that you will provide him in the first few years of his life.

Easing Your Baby into the New World

When your baby first arrives, he sees himself as an extension of you. He doesn't yet have an awareness of himself as an independent person. He reaches for you, cries for you, and longs to snuggle against your body. You are his safe space, and you will continue to play this role for his whole life, even as his world expands and grows.

Carrying your baby

During the first two or three months, go with your baby's cues. Dr. Harvey Karp calls this period the "fourth trimester" (see Chapter 2) for a reason. The baby is just getting used to the world outside the womb and needs to be coddled, held, and comforted as much as possible. As often as you can, try to replicate that safe, warm place by keeping him swaddled, holding him close to your body, and feeding him frequently. Be gentle when you expand his world. Go slow, be deliberate, and be consistent.

Start by using the car seat or stroller only for transit, not as a carrier. Some parents have the tendency to put the baby in the car seat, drive to the destination, and keep the baby in the car seat during the event. In this situation, the baby doesn't experience any new interactions through physical or motor activity. He just stays in his chair and watches the world instead of interacting with it. Sometimes, of course, taking him out of his seat isn't possible; keeping the baby strapped in is the most efficient option. However, if you can, take him out. Slings and wraps allow him to feel you, hear your heartbeat, and be held close to you in a way that car seats can't. Plastic isn't nurturing; a body is.

When you take your baby out of his seat, let him touch something new or look at the world from a new angle. Put him on your lap, or, when he's older, in a highchair. The new perspective will assure him that you enjoy having him participate in your world.

Expanding your baby's world

Begin to expand your baby's world by talking about his body instead of examining transient objects such as trees, cars, and the grass. Things in the wider world are not permanent and will not always be there to talk about. Noticing these types of objects and recalling them require *object permanence* (the ability to recognize that when something is gone it will come back), a skill that isn't developed until the age of 6 to 12 months. That does not mean that you shouldn't talk about the world around you; you definitely should! But don't worry about teaching all the details. There will be plenty of time for that.

Focus on his body parts, which are always there no matter what environment he's in. Gently touch his nose, mouth, arms, and legs and tell him, "These are your arms! This is your nose. You have a mouth too!" Keep your tone happy and engaged. Your baby loves to hear your voice, and most babies love to be touched, so the combination is irresistible to him.

Gently move your baby's arms and legs as you talk about them. My son, even at two months, loved to move his arms and legs. So my husband started this game, which my son still loves at two years and even plays with his baby sister. We placed him on his back and moved his legs in a bicycle motion, saying "Run! Run!" Next, we placed his hands on his chest one after the other saying, "Arms, arms!" Finally, we touched his nose and said, "Nose!" He dissolved in laughter, and still does, every single time.

Begin to expand your baby's world by talking about his body.

You can also stroke your baby's cheek or hair. One rule: No tickling. This applies also to an older infant or toddler. Tickling places a baby in a position of no control and of extreme vulnerability. He may be laughing, but that's because he doesn't know what else to do. Holding him down to tickle him is an absolute no-no. It creates a feeling of powerlessness; you are so much bigger than him, and he has no control over when it stops. It's not a good idea to play games that promote one powerful player and one powerless player. Instead, stick to gentler activities.

Physical and Motor Skills during the First Three Years

There is so much to see and celebrate as your baby grows. Keep in mind that there is a wide range in the development of physical and motor skills. Children will reach the common physical and motor milestones at their own pace. Try not to worry if your toddler takes a longer time to become steady on his feet, even if his friends are running around in circles. Each child has his own strengths and challenges. If you do have any major concerns, you can always discuss them with your child's pediatrician.

The first year: From head control to crawling

In the beginning, your infant will rely on his reflexes. Although he cannot hold his head up on his own, he may wrap his whole hand around your finger or a piece of your hair, and you'll be amazed at his strength! But he's not doing this on purpose. Clinging onto something is a safety reflex for him, and it gives him a feeling of comfort. This will eventually become a conscious choice, but for now, it's just a protective reflex.

Your newborn cannot roll over, sit up, or voluntarily change position, so be very aware of how you position your infant, and move him when he seems unhappy. He will need lots of help sitting up and looking around. When he wants to look around, he will be happy for you to hold his head and neck with one hand and support his back with the other. Alternatively, carry him over your shoulder so he can see the world as it passes. Place him on his back to sleep; this is the safest position for his regulated breathing and is recommended by the American Academy of Pediatrics (AAP) as a prevention of Sudden Infant Death Syndrome (SIDS). Keep all pillows and blankets away from your sleeping baby. If these get in the way of his breathing, he doesn't yet have the skills to remove them and could suffocate. Instead, use an infant sleep sack (a wearable blanket) to keep him warm, says the AAP.

This newborn phase doesn't last long. By two to three months, your infant may start trying to roll over on his own. You might place him on his side and see him try to kick furiously to get onto his back. He may even be able to roll from his back to his side.

Place him on his stomach each day for a few minutes so that he can practice lifting his head and moving his body. But don't be surprised if he protests and cries. This can be a very frustrating position for an infant! Redirect him by giving him a colorful toy to look at or a mirror so he can study his reflection, or have another family member crouch low and make silly facial expressions at his eye level. If he's really unhappy, start by just resting him on your chest on his tummy so that he can listen to your heartbeat.

Place your baby on his stomach each day for a few minutes so that he can practice lifting his head and moving his body.

As he becomes more comfortable, put him on his stomach on a blanket or an activity mat that provides visual stimulation. This *tummy time* will increase the strength in his neck and back, help his vision because he'll see the world from a different perspective, and help him focus on close objects, preparing him for crawling. Babies who are given regular opportunities to practice tummy time enjoy additional benefits such as developing earlier head control and crawling and earlier and stronger motor skills.

Once your infant starts to show stronger head control, around three or four months, you can start helping him practice to sit up. Begin by laying him on his back, and then slowly hold his wrists (or continue to support the back of his neck if he needs it) and gently guide him to a sitting position. When you get him to a seated position, prop him up with a nursing pillow or a few sofa pillows. Infant chairs with adjustable backs are excellent aids at this point in an infant's physical development. You can adjust him to more and more of a seated position as he becomes more comfortable with being seated at a proper angle. By five or six months, he may be able to support himself while sitting, for a short while. He may, after a few seconds, tip to the side, which is why the pillows are still helpful! Most likely, his lower spine will still need a bit of support for a few more weeks.

The next major motor milestone is crawling, but some babies use rolling as a way to get around instead of crawling. Once he's figured out how to roll, be ready for him to roll all around the room! You may find your little one under a table or in a tiny corner. Some babies rely on rolling for months, whereas others do it for a short time or not at all and quickly replace it with crawling. And while some babies reach this milestone by seven or eight months, others don't crawl until they're almost a year old. But if your baby has had regular tummy time, he's had the chance to practice lifting his head and eventually his arms and legs, which strengthened them for crawling.

Sometimes, parents try to skip the crawling stage and encourage the baby to walk early. It's very important *not* to do this. Crawling is a crucial developmental step because it encourages hand-eye coordination, balance, spatial and kinesthetic awareness, and tactile input. Additionally, in order for a baby to crawl, he needs to move his right hand and left knee together, and then follow it with the left hand and right knee. Researchers have explained that this movement activates "the fibers in the corpus callosum that connect the brain's left and right hemispheres . . . the better developed these fibers are, the better connected the two hemispheres will be, enabling faster communication between the left and right sides of the brain." Crawling is an incredibly important stage for brain development, and should not be skipped if at all possible. Some babies don't crawl at all and still do just fine developmentally, but if your baby is using crawling as a way to move forward in his motor development, allow him to do so. Be patient and encourage him to grow at his own pace.

By the time your baby does start crawling, make sure you've baby-proofed your home. See the sidebar for some guidelines. And remember that all babies develop on their own time with motor skills. My son actually crawled backward for a few weeks before he learned that he could go forward too!

A Tip from Sarahlynne

Baby-proofing Your Home

- **Perform a pre-baby inspection.** Before your baby arrives, take a walk around your house and look at it from a baby's perspective. Don't forget about the outside of the house. Does your deck have railings? Could a baby fall through them? You don't need to have your deck reconstructed, but this kind of walk will help you decide on solutions, such as adding netting before your baby is crawling and wants to explore outside.
- **Emphasize safety.** By the rolling and crawling stage, be sure that your house is baby-proofed, blocking electrical outlets, installing baby gates, and moving dangerous objects and cleaning supplies out of reach. Your baby will be curious to explore everything in the room. See that electrical outlet over there? He thinks it's a toy. He'll also be so busy moving that he won't heed his direction and can easily fall down stairs.
- **Check furniture.** When your baby is standing, consider securing furniture to the wall, especially if he can get out of his crib or is left alone in his room. He could try to pull himself up on a dresser or bookshelf, and if it isn't secure, it could topple on him and cause serious injury. Even very heavy furniture can fall if pulled from a certain angle.
- **Resist the urge to buy a baby walker.** Walkers can be dangerous because they make it easier for babies to get around faster, touch things that are particularly dangerous, or even fall down the stairs. Furthermore, a baby using a walker won't be doing as much to strengthen his muscles. Instead, get your child a toy he can push around, and encourage him by praising him, clapping for him, and celebrating his efforts.
- **Maintain all baby appliances.** When he is cruising or walking, make sure the gates that you have installed are working effectively. Gates and safety precautions such as locking cabinets and covering sharp edges are a must at this stage.

The second year: Cruising and walking

Once your baby feels confident crawling, he'll try to pull himself up to a standing position. He may wobble and wiggle on his legs, as this is the first time he's ever had to support his full body weight. He cannot take charge of his legs until he has control over his back and hips. At this point, he'll start to stand in his crib, pulling himself up and "bouncing" up and down. Once he's got himself sturdy (this could take many tries and possibly weeks!), he'll begin to "cruise," or move or slide his legs sideways, balancing himself with the walls, furniture, toys, or anything that can help him hold himself up. One of the great things about this phase is that he won't be interested in too many toys; standing and cruising will provide immense entertainment, and he will work on these skills all the time, sometimes even in the middle of the night!

Some babies will not walk independently until well into their second year, and that's perfectly normal. A baby may start walking anytime between 9 and 18 months and may still be cruising as late as 15 months. It's all completely normal. You can encourage your baby to begin walking as soon as he has become more steady on his feet and more comfortable balancing in a standing position.

To encourage your child to "cruise" and later walk, put a toy in front of him and ask him to try to reach it. Help him when he needs it; don't let him get too frustrated, but encourage and motivate him too. Help him feel the floor by allowing him to play in bare feet whenever possible. Play a simplistic version of "tag," where you stand only a few steps in front of him and encourage him to "get you" by taking a few paces. Give him a huge hug when he reaches you and collapses into your arms with laughter and pride.

Stand a few steps in front of your baby and encourage her to get to you by taking a few paces.

When your baby first learns to walk, be prepared to chase him around for the next six months or so. Walking is providing him so much stimulation that he doesn't have any control over where he's going. He probably won't listen when you tell him to turn around or walk in a different direction. He's too busy practicing this awesome new skill and doesn't care where he's walking. Furthermore, he's so focused on moving his feet that he probably doesn't even see certain objects or furniture until he falls into them! However, he has understood the word "no" since nine months, so feel free to use that as he ambles around the world and gets steady on his feet.

If you don't want your toddler to walk in a certain direction, get down to his level, turn his body around, and say, "Come this way." If he's touching something that is dangerous, again, get down to his level and tell him, "This is not for babies," or "This is not for you," and then pick him up and move him to a new location or divert his attention to something new. Research has shown that at this stage your baby is very aware of where you are, even if it doesn't seem that way. In fact, he probably won't ever venture farther than 200 feet away from you while he's still feeling unsteady.

During this delicate phase, teach your toddler to turn around and crawl backward down the stairs instead of walking down. It's much safer for him. Later, when he's physically ready, he can walk down stairs.

Once your toddler is more comfortable on his feet, start to give him simple directions such as "Stay with me," "Hold my hand," or "Turn around and come back." Begin to teach him safety skills when you cross the street or walk in a parking lot. However, continue to give him many chances to walk and play freely in safe areas such as fields of grass, playgrounds, and gated rooms in the house.

Even if he has been walking awhile, don't be surprised if he asks you to carry him when you move away from him too quickly. This is a self-preservation technique; he knows he cannot keep up with you, and, wanting to feel safe, he'll plead with you to pick him up. He's still learning how to use his muscles in this huge way and isn't necessarily ready to understand what it means to follow you when you ask, keep up with you, or move in the direction you choose. But keep using this new vocabulary, because eventually he'll understand and start listening and following directions.

Climbing may be a huge pastime of your toddler as well. When my son turned 18 months, he wanted to climb on and out of everything—the sofas, the chairs, his crib—and up and down the stairs. Most of the time, I was terrified he was going to end up in the emergency room. As an outlet for his energy, I started taking him to toddler gym classes, took him outside on most days, made indoor forts with pillows for climbing, and began setting boundaries with him on what he wasn't allowed to do inside.

The third year: Running, climbing, and jumping

For months, walking was enough for your toddler. But soon, he'll discover what his legs can really do! This is the time he'll run, climb higher, move in circles, jump, bounce, kick balls, and dance. He'll love playing with balls and playing tag, and will benefit from physical games such as "Red light, green light" (modified for his ability to follow directions), "Musical chairs," and "Ring-around-the-rosy."

What NOW?

Music that Encourages Movement in Your Infant and Toddler

- *Coconut Grove* by In the Nick of Time
- *Enchanting Original Songs for All the Family* by Zootopia
- *Small People* by Tumble Tots
- *Wiggle, Wiggle, and Other Exercises* by Bobby Susser Songs for Children

At this stage, he will move purposefully and predictably, so give him opportunities to use his new skills. He can help you empty the dishwasher, bring his plate to the sink, or help make the bed. All of these activities will help him practice fine-motor control (moving his fingers in purposeful ways) as he also practices his gross-motor control, such as walking and running.

You'll be able to give him more freedoms in public places, trusting him to stay with you while you run short errands at the post office or bank without a stroller. He now has the ability to know when he needs to hold your hand, when he can walk freely next to you, and when he needs to sit in his stroller. But he still needs lots of time to practice all these new physical movements, so be sure to give him many chances to dance, kick, throw and roll balls, run, skip, slide down slides, swing on swings, and climb play structures.

Sensory Experiences during the First Three Years

When my son was very small, he used to stare at the ceiling fan. He loved watching it spin around and around. It was an amazing sensory experience for him. Sensory interactions come from things you may not expect. The whole world is new to your baby, so everything is fascinating! In the first few years, you can take advantage of this and, with very few toys and little technology, amuse your child for hours.

Just as physical and motor movement are critical to development, so are sensory experiences. Child development researcher Jill Stamm explains, "All of a child's future skills—tying a shoe, being able to use a pencil easily, swinging on a swing—are complex processes that rely on a strong foundation of the brain's ability to incorporate sensory input." This is because every second, two million new pieces of information enter the central nervous system first! The central nervous system (the brain and spinal cord) is responsible for the processing of the entire nervous system, controlling how our bodies automatically respond to situations.

Your baby's earliest sensory encounters

Sensory experiences include all interactions that invite at least one of the five senses: sight, smell, sound, taste, and touch. Encourage your child to experience the world through his senses whenever possible. Invite him to touch a new object, smell a flower, look at a building, or listen to a new sound. You're probably already doing this automatically. When my son was less than a year old, I explained to one of my friends how hard it was to put on a huge Rosh Hashanah meal and lamented that he wouldn't even remember any of the details.

"But he will," she advised. "Fill the house with the smells of the challah bread and the sweet sauce you make to go with the chicken. He may not remember the holidays, but those smells will become an indelible piece of his childhood."

Our day-to-day interactions form what our children will look back on as a childhood, and sensory encounters are a huge part of that. So, if years from now, the smell of baking challah evokes a reaction in my children, I'll know why, and it'll make me feel proud and happy.

Here's something even stranger. When I was pregnant with my son, I danced in a Zumba class twice a week. The instructor always played a slow "cha-cha" in the middle of the class, and it was the same beautiful, melodic song each week. I downloaded it and listened to it at home as well. A few days after my son was born, when he was crying I put on the song. He immediately calmed down.

As astounding as this experience was to me, it's actually rooted in research. It has been documented that crying newborns who listen to a tune they "heard" in the womb begin to quickly calm down! In fact, other studies have shown that newborns prefer their mother's voice to all others, perhaps because they've had so much experience with her voice and heartbeat in utero. Sensory experiences start prior to birth, and these familiarities can comfort a scared and overwhelmed infant in his early weeks.

Giving your baby a chance to use his five senses may seem easy and obvious. But in our world filled with TV, computers, and mobile devices, it's more challenging than it seems. However, a variety of sensory experiences will give his brain a chance to sort the information into appropriate "file drawers," creating background schema (see Chapter 1). So when you can, give your baby an opportunity to see the world through all of his senses. The sensory activities at the end of this chapter will show you additional ways to stimulate all of your baby's senses and encourage cognitive and emotional development.

Touch: The most important sensory experience

Although the other sensory experiences are important, touch is by far the most crucial in an infant's development. Actually, the mouth is the most sensitive of all the touch organs, which is why your baby loves to put everything in his mouth!

Touch is such a sacred and human biological need that children who have gone a long time without physical touch and comfort have been diagnosed with *failure to thrive.* Failure to thrive, a condition recognized by a lack of growth, can be brought on by poor nutrition but also by lack of human contact. Heart-breaking examples of child institutions in the early twentieth century showed devastating results in children who were lacking emotional care. In these extreme circumstances in which young kids weren't ever held or loved, they cried for hours, became depressed, refused to eat, lost weight, and stopped growing. Eventually, many died. Years later, when hospitals began using physical contact as part of their treatment plans for children, the child mortality rate dropped from 30% to 10%.

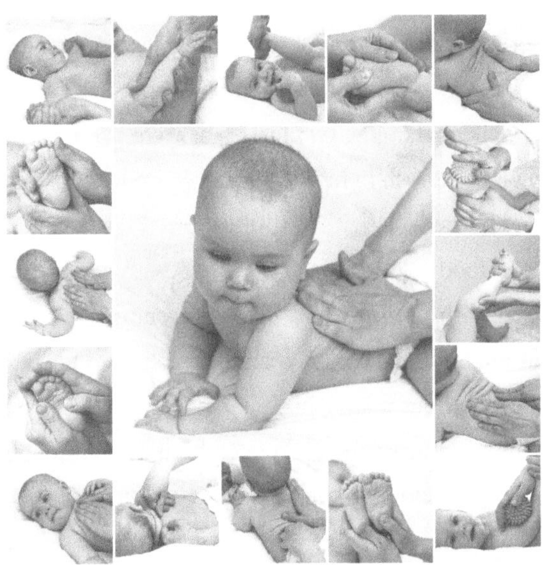

Touch is by far the most crucial sensory experience in an infant's development. Infant massage is shown here.

Infants and toddlers long to be held. It provides them safety, warmth, security, and love. That's why intentional touch, including infant massage, is an easy way to touch and bond with your infant (see Chapter 2).

Parents naturally encourage a newborn to build his sense of touch and to connect touch with love and comfort. For example, snuggling with him and allowing him to hear and feel your heartbeat are reminiscent of the womb, his coziest place. As an infant grows, he'll reach for his caregiver when he's hurt or sad, knowing that physical touch will comfort him. And a toddler will run to his caregiver when he's scared, nervous, shy, or hurt, because he knows that the feeling of arms around him will provide him with security.

What to do when everything goes in the mouth

Beyond basic physical contact, there are tons of fun experiences that involve various textures. However, encouraging your child to touch and feel new things can pose some dangers. You may be afraid to introduce items like sensory boxes and glue sticks because you know your baby will put everything straight into his mouth. I totally get that. My son, even as he turned two, was notorious for trying to taste everything (except for new foods, but that's a different story!). One day, we went over to a friend's house where we were going to paint with liquid sidewalk chalk. The two little girls were painting on the pavement. My son immediately put the brush in his mouth and started licking it.

I tore the brush away from him and blurted, "What's in this stuff?"

My friend laughed. "Cornstarch and food coloring."

So I get it. You may not want to play with a sensory box, Play-Doh, crayons, dirt, or mulch. It may terrify you to go near anything that could possibly be a hazard to your baby, because he'll see something new and put it straight in his mouth. (Remember, the mouth is the most sensitive of all the touch organs!) Young children go through a phase of development, especially when they're teething, where it seems that every object goes into their mouth. This is a combination of exploring new textures in every way possible and experimenting with what can soothe aching gums. During this phase, it's probably wise to limit some of the sensory activities that require smaller pieces or inedible materials. Here are some strategies to deal with your baby's tendency to put everything in the mouth:

- **Offer consistent direction.** Every time your child puts something inappropriate in his mouth, tell him, "Not in your mouth," and then show him by gently taking his hand away from his mouth. It's important to always put a physical gesture with a verbal direction so your child can understand what you mean. This gives the child two ways to understand one request.
- **Use a pacifier.** While my son was deep in this phase (around 12 to 14 months), I let him have a pacifier while he was playing with sand or dirt. That way, he was soothing his gums but still getting the opportunity to explore new textures. However, as soon as this phase passed, the pacifier went back to the crib for nighttime use only.
- **Give him other alternatives.** For example, "Sand does not go in your mouth, but you can bite on this teething toy." Keep these teething alternatives ready in case he seems to want to chew on something inappropriate.
- **Check to see if your baby is hungry!** Once, at about 20 months, my son put a handful of dirt in his mouth. When I went over to tell him no, he put his fingers to his mouth and said, "Eat! Eat!" Of course, we gave him a snack immediately!
- **Use consequences.** When your toddler gets older, around two or three, you can institute a consequence for when he tries to taste something inappropriate. Give one warning, and then take the item away or put it in "time out."

Giving your child the chance to experience the world through his body, his movements, and his senses is a wonderful gift. Go at his pace and look at the world through his eyes. You'll be amazed at the things you make take for granted that are new to him; simplistic things that, to your baby, are tantalizing and exhilarating.

Activities to Stimulate Physical and Motor Skills in Your Baby

When you're choosing which physical and motor activities to perform with your baby, be aware of the stage he's in. Opt for an activity that will give him confidence in a familiar skill or practice a new one.

Activities for Ages 0–6 Months

- **Kisses everywhere.** Give your baby kisses all over his body.
- **Whispering.** Simply whisper in his ear.
- **Body boogie.** Touch each of his body parts and tell him the name of each. Do the same to yourself. For example, "This is my arm and this is your arm!" Move his legs and then his arms up and down and back and forth. Tell him what you're doing while you do it; alternate fast and slow.
- **Chore helper.** Carry him around while you do your daily chores. He'll love bouncing in your arms or in his carrier and will find peace in the rhythm of your movements.
- **Copying your facial expressions.** With a baby as young as six weeks old, you can stick out your tongue and your baby may copy you! Once he starts to smile, you can smile at him when he smiles at you. As he gets older, you can make more facial movements for him to try to copy, like the fish face, making raspberries with your tongue, or smacking your lips together.
- **Baby yoga.** Get into a downward dog position and put your baby on the floor underneath you. He'll love looking at you in this new direction. Or put him on the floor underneath you and do pushups. As you lower yourself to the floor and lift yourself back up again, he'll enjoy seeing your face close and far away. You can even kiss his tummy as you lower yourself down. Bonus: This one is a mommy or daddy workout!
- **"Helicopter."** Put him above your head and slowly rotate him, saying "helicopter" in a happy voice. As he gets older, he may want to open his arms out like wings. (Wait until your baby has firm head control before trying this one.)
- **Graduating to toys.** Once he's starting to sit up on his own, prop him up with some pillows and give him a toy to hold.

Activities for Ages 6 Months and Older

- Parent trampoline. Let him jump and crawl on you while you pretend to be overtaken by him. He'll find it hilarious.
- Dance. Turn on the music and start dancing. Copy his moves or have him copy yours. A younger infant may just raise his arms up and down, while a toddler may turn in circles. Both will enjoy watching you mimic the movements.
- Hiding games. Play peekaboo with your hands, or with an older infant, play a game when he crawls behind a piece of furniture. When my son was crawling, he used to go behind the kitchen island, and I would say, "Where are you?" He would laugh hysterically and crawl over to me.

- Cushion island. Pull the couch cushions off and place them on the floor. Spread out a variety of items such as toys, utensils, blankets, shoes, and hats. The cushionless couch is the island, the floor is the water, and your child has to gather items he'll need on the island by stepping from cushion to cushion. This is a playful way to figure out how to use that toddler body. (Kate Delaney Bailey, occupational therapist and mother of two)
- Exercise with Mommy or Daddy. Lie on the floor, look at each other, and say, "One, Two, Three!" Then, do a situp and invite him to roll himself up and copy you.
- Simple movements. A walking toddler who can follow simple directions will love games that let him copy you. Stand up, sit down, put your hands on your head, and spin in a circle. Say these directions as you make the movements. Once your toddler learns to jump, add that to the game. You can make it more advanced by adding directions such as "left, right" or turning it into "Heads, Shoulders, Knees, and Toes." Expand this into "Simon says" or "Red light, green light" as he's ready.
- Dive bomb. When you change the bed, pile all the comforters, pillows, and blankets into a huge pile. Give your toddler a running start, and have him run into the pile and jump on top.
- Animal walks. Do a "penguin walk" with feet together and hands down, an "elephant walk" with one arm pretending to be a long snout, or march, lifting your knees high. So simple. Endless fun.
- Fun walking. Practice walking on tiptoe, walking backward, or doing a "crab walk."
- Car dance. At a red light or stop sign, turn around and show him dance moves he can do with the music. Wiggle your shoulders, "raise the roof," or bop your head. For a younger baby, you could sing a song with motions, such as "The Itsy-Bitsy Spider."
- Body tracing. Have him lie down on a long piece of butcher paper. Trace his body outline. Then, have him color in his clothes and draw his face. He'll enjoy this life-size art activity, and it will help him be more aware of his clothes and body. This one also works well with chalk in the driveway. Put a blockade at the driveway's entrance as a safety precaution.
- Freeze dance. Freeze dancing can be fun for the whole family. Play some music and have everyone dance around. When the music stops, everyone freezes and says, "Shh!" placing their finger to their lips.
- Cardboard tunnel. Make a tunnel out of large boxes. He can crawl through, hide, or jump in and out of them.
- Vehicle slide. Put a car or truck on top of an outdoor slide. Have your child try to catch it as you send it down for a ride.

Sensory Activities for Your Baby

Remember to do these activities one at a time; you don't want to overstimulate your baby, especially when he's very young. Choose an age-appropriate activity. Watch his cues. When he turns his head away, he's done with that activity and is asking for it to be over. And remember, some children have very high sensitivities to certain sounds, tastes, or textures. If your baby is showing extreme distaste or anxiety toward a certain activity, immediately stop. Do not force him to participate. Most likely, he is not being stubborn; instead, he's feeling overwhelmed, anxious, or scared. Do you have any sounds or tastes that make your skin crawl? So does your baby!

Activities for Ages 0–1

- **The first few minutes of life.** If at all possible, the nurse or doctor will place a newborn on his mother's chest. This is because the baby will find the most comfort in snuggling with his mother, listening to the voice and heartbeat that has kept him safe and secure all these months. The baby may even naturally find his way to the breast and begin suckling. His natural instinct is to snuggle and be comforted by touch. Hold him, stroke him, nurse him if you choose to, but keep him with you within the first few hours of his life. Continue to kiss, hold, and cuddle with him as much as you can during the next several months. (Nursing and bottle-feeding provide great opportunities for hugs and soft touch.) You can never give a baby too many snuggles!
- Black-and-white patterns. A newborn's eyes are not yet fully developed for long distance and color detail, but he loves the stark contrast of light and dark colors and will be fascinated by black and white patterns. Attach a drawing to the side of his bassinet or crib and he will be riveted by the details.
- Singing. Even if you can't sing, sing to your baby anyway. He'll love the melodies and sooner than you think, he will begin to "expect" certain parts of the song. It amazed me how early my son said his version of "e-i-e-i-o" when I sang "Old McDonald Had a Farm." If you don't know any songs, sing the basics: "Twinkle, Twinkle, Little Star," the alphabet song, or "Do-Re-Me." The baby will love the melody, no matter the words.
- Home tour. Carry your baby around your home facing away from you and stop to talk about each item you see. Talk in a soothing voice about various details for each stop on your tour. For example, "That is called a vase. It is made of glass. The glass is clear so you can see through it. We use the vase to hold flowers. These flowers are blue and yellow. They smell very nice." (Kate Delaney Bailey, occupational therapist and mother of two)

- Baby massage. Research has shown that the more an infant is touched, the more he'll learn about the world! See the activities in Chapter 2 for a description of infant massage.
- Varied textures. Allow him to smell, see, and touch various materials. Give him things that go "crunch!" or "squish!" or "crinkle!"
- Towel taps. Gently tap his mouth with a soft cloth. Do this slowly, and then quickly. Watch his responses. If he smiles, he's finding it quite entertaining!
- Spider walk. Walk your fingers up his tummy and chest as you say the words "fast" and "slow." Alternate your speed to accompany the words.
- Scarf play. For infants past five months, put a scarf over your face and have him pull it off, or put a scarf on his face (when he's ready; see-through scarves work the best) and pull it off or have him pull it off. While you are playing this game, say lines like, "Where are you? I can see you!" This game helps him with object permanence, the skill of knowing an object will come back after it disappears.
- Mirror play. Put him in front of a mirror and ask him who he sees. At first, he'll be mystified at the person staring back at him, but eventually, he'll figure it out and will be so excited! He may kiss, hug, or make faces in the mirror. Make a silly face and have your baby copy you.
- Food play. This one is messy, but is so much fun for your baby. Let him play with his food. Before feeding him with a spoon, allow him to get his fingers into his puree, spread it out on his tray and maybe even taste it.
- Shower fun. This one works only for babies who can sit well on their own. Put him in the shower with you. Sit him down, and sit with him. Let the water "rain" on him, feel the water as it puddles at your feet, and allow him to feel it on his face and body.

Activities for Ages 1–3

- Pudding painting. Prepare instant vanilla pudding and make sure it's thick. Drop dollops on a cookie sheet and add drops of food coloring for finger painting. Invite your child to mix and play with the colors. Best of all, it's edible! (Anne D., preschool educator and grandmother)
- Sensory box. Place beads, lentils, sand, small toy trucks, and other objects with various textures into a shoebox. Allow him to explore these textures and use his imagination. (If your baby puts everything in his mouth, try other types of sensory boxes. For example, a big water bucket filled with boats and bath toys, a sand table filled with big trucks, plastic sieves, shovels, and buckets are excellent alternatives.)

(continued)

- Flashlight fun. Take your toddler into a small room with you and turn off the lights. Then, shine a flashlight on various objects in the room (if you're in the bathroom, you can shine on the toilet, sink, and towels). Point out each object and name it. Next, use the flashlight to light up and name each part of the body. Be sure to give him some free time with the flashlight too! (Mary G., mother of two)
- Fruit shapes. Give your toddler some soft fruit, such as bananas and strawberries, and a plastic knife. Sit with him as he cuts the fruit. (Mary G., mother of two)
- Shaking bottle. Fill an old water bottle with colored water and a solid such as glitter, marbles, rocks, leaves, or rice. Hot-glue the top on so he can't unscrew it. Allow him to shake, twist, and roll the bottle, watching the contents swirl and wiggle. (Mary G., mother of two)
- Stickers, Play-Doh, and coloring. Toddlers have a blast with these. (Watch him; stickers are choking hazards!)
- Makeup. Give him your powder compact and a makeup brush and "pretend" to put on makeup. You don't even have to open the compact. The brush feels soft on his skin, and it's a great imagination activity.
- Kitchen cleanup. Put plastic toys or kitchen plasticware into a clean kitchen sink full of soapy water. Give your toddler sponges and towels for drying. Some good clean fun will be had by all! (Kate Delaney Bailey, occupational therapist and mother of two)
- Water fun. Try a variety of activities depending on your baby's comfort, age, and skill levels:
    - When your baby is small, drizzle some water on him while he is in the bath. When he gets older, give him some buckets or cups to fill up and dump out.
    - Even when he's not in the bath, have fun with water. Let him stand on a stool, fill the sink a few inches, and let him splash around. Give him some plastic containers to fill and dump in the sink.
    - You can even use the dishwasher door if you don't mind a bit of a wet mess. Open the dishwasher and fill up the door basin with a few inches of water. Give him measuring cups and buckets to scoop the water. It'll be right at his level!
    - Make colorful ice by adding food coloring to the ice cubes in your ice tray. Place them in the bath with your baby and have him track them with his eyes as they float around the water. As he gets older and more confident in the bathtub, he can try to reach for them before they melt. As he begins to understand varying colors, encourage his detective skills by asking him to find a particular color ice cube.
- Makeshift musical instruments. There are so many ways your little one can make some noise!
    - Bang a wooden spoon on a pot.
    - Shake boxes of macaroni and cheese.

- Gently tap the side of a glass with a spoon.
- Play with volume. Have him bang loudly and softly.
- Play with his voice as a musical instrument, too. If he screams (which most toddlers do just to practice their voice volume), teach him how to "silent" scream, with no sound. These games teach him that he has control over his volume.

- Stacking cups. Put nesting cups in a row and place a ball underneath one. Quickly move the cups around and see if he can guess where the ball is. Allow him to stack and unstack the cups.
- Sand experiments. If you don't have a sandbox, fill a shallow plastic bowl or cookie sheet with some sand, sugar, Rice Krispies, or oats. Let him run his hands through it, fill cups, and dump them out.
- Guess the hand. Place a small object in one hand and close both fists. Have him try to guess where the object is. Open one hand to reveal the hidden object. Then switch up your hands and try again. Don't worry about being too secretive about this game; he'll try to follow where the object goes!
- Ice surprises. Freeze a few small plastic toys in ice cubes. Give your child the ice cubes and talk about ways to melt the ice and get the toys. You can put the ice cubes in a bath of warm water and watch the ice melt away. Watch your child closely, since small toys can be choking hazards.
- Brown bag guess. Put a bunch of different textured items into a brown bag, like a feather, a rock, a piece of paper, and a sticker. Have your child reach in and guess what he's touching before he pulls it out. This one works well for an older toddler who can verbalize his thoughts.
- Liquid sidewalk chalk. Mix some cornstarch, water, and food coloring together to form the chalk. This makes a great precursor to sidewalk chalk. Fill up an egg carton with various colors and give your child a paintbrush, or let her use her hands to paint the driveway.
- Moon sand. Mix two cups of flour and a quarter cup of baby oil. Give your toddler shovels and buckets and pretend you're at the beach.

Chapter Preview

- Why parentese is so beneficial
- Helping your child develop stronger language skills
- The benefits of sign language
- How to raise a bilingual baby
- Language-building activities for your baby

Chapter 4

The Secret to Strong Language Development (It's Not What You Think!)

Is a baby born with a preference for certain voices? Absolutely! The research shows that babies begin their language acquisition "in the last trimester of pregnancy, when the unborn child hears his mother's voice and becomes familiar with the sound patterns of her language." So even if you aren't talking directly to your baby while you're pregnant, she's hearing your voice all day, and these reassuring rhythms will make her feel happy and comforted after she's born.

Actually, newborns can detect even more than voice. In one study, pregnant women read a passage to their babies in utero. After these babies were born and they heard the practiced passages in addition to new ones, data showed that they preferred the familiar passages over brand new ones. These results confirmed the researcher's hypothesis that "prenatal auditory experience can influence postnatal auditory preferences." The babies recognized and preferred familiar over novel experiences. This study began to confirm that infants will react well to words, phrases, and voices that they've already heard. So talking and singing to your baby, starting during pregnancy, will comfort her and ease her stress after she's born.

The Benefits of Parentese

When we talk to our infants, we automatically change our tone and cadence. It's amazing how naturally we use that singsong, slow tone that we'd never use with anyone else. In the words of language development experts, "Adults the world over tend to talk to babies face-to-face, in a high-pitched, singsong, repetitive manner, with elongated vowels, engaging intonation, and emphasis on key words." That tone is *parentese*. Most parents talk to their babies this way, and it's been proven to have strong, positive effects. Slower, stretched out sentences help your baby distinguish not only the sounds of the words but also the breaks between words. Because infants don't have control over their entire vocal range but can repeat sounds at higher pitches, talking to your child in a higher pitch will help her more easily copy your sounds.

But parentese is not baby talk. It's important to always model well-spoken English. Your baby will imitate what you say, so you want her to hear the correct version of every word.

Do mothers and fathers speak the same parentese?

Within months of being born, thanks to your parentese, your baby begins to figure out what sounds to make, how to elicit responses, and how to take part in conversation. Talking to your baby from the start is important, but there's so much more that you can do. A huge part of her language conceptualization has to do with how her caregivers handle the first three years. From an infant's earliest months, she needs to hear a wide-ranging vocabulary and sentences that are structured in a variety of ways. But it's easier than you may think.

Men and women are naturally inclined to talk to their children differently, which can contribute to the child having more opportunities at diverse language. For example, mothers are more likely to ask yes/no questions and will use more supportive and positive language than fathers, but they are less likely to use informative language, which seems to come more naturally to fathers. These unique interactions are excellent for the baby's language development. In a crucial study in this area, researchers commented, "Fathers' language input to their children at 24 months of age made a unique contribution to children's later expressive language skills at 36 months of age after parent education and quality of child care was considered." If a child is hearing more than one parent's style of talking to her, she'll learn more ways to understand and express her thoughts.

Socioeconomic levels excellent child care, and parent education can also be key to a young child's opportunities to hear varied language. In the same study, researchers commented that parents at higher socioeconomic levels use a "richer vocabulary of object labels" and can therefore contribute to a more expansive vocabulary and sentence structure base for their young child. The researchers also found that "young children in higher quality child care have stronger receptive and expressive skills." Furthermore, fathers "who used a greater number of different *word roots* during free play situations had children who had more advanced expressive language skills one year later."

What is a *word root*? It's a word or part of a word that establishes meaning, or is used to build the rest of the word. For example, the root *auto* means "self." So "automobile" (a car that has its own engine) and "autograph" (one's own signature) are both in the same category of the root *auto*. A baby who hears these categorized words will see the similarities, especially if, when she is older, they are pointed out. For now, she'll just see the commonalities in the words and use them in her own vocabulary. The fathers in this study used this varied vocabulary during free play; there was no formal instruction, and yet it still made a huge difference in their children's expressive language.

Balancing act: When to talk and when to be quiet

Often, we hear that it's so important to talk to our babies all the time. And indeed, it is the child's participation in engaging conversation, not how much language she overhears, that matters. However, as the strongest research shows, it is important that children hear more words *as well as* a greater variety of words from their earliest months. Some experts describe this as "the power of play talk."

But before you start worrying that you're not talking to your child enough, or that she's not hearing enough variation in language, keep in mind a great secret about language development in babies: *Talking to them is important, but it's only a piece of the puzzle and not necessarily the most critical piece.* Surprising, isn't it? It's not necessary for you to chat to your baby all day long. She needs a break from all the stimulation in order to synthesize everything around her. When you take her for a walk, sometimes show her the sights, but other times let her just quietly observe. If you notice her deep in play, try not to interrupt her to ask, "What are you doing?" I learned this the hard way. My son used to love playing with all the fun, colorful animals in his bouncer. He'd jump and play independently and happily. However, as soon as I began communicating with him, asking him, "What are you doing? Is that a monkey?" he'd lose his train of thought and all of a sudden become very frustrated because he wanted my full attention, now that he remembered I was there. I think he felt interrupted and couldn't get his focus back.

Read the situation. If your baby is happily playing, step back and let her explore. If she seems to want to engage, talk to her. A baby who wants to chat will look at you, smile, laugh, or start fussing. A baby who is deep in thought may be completely engrossed in looking out the window, playing with her toys, or just observing what's going on around her. Following her signals will give her the perfect amount of language and the perfect amount of "down time."

How Language Develops during the First Three Years

It's important to understand the stages your child goes through as she picks up the language around her, develops conceptual understanding, and begins to express her own thoughts—all of which happen earlier than you may think. Remember that every child develops differently. The range of language development, like that of physical and motor skills, is wide. Some children will accomplish certain language milestones earlier than others. These differences do not necessarily point to developmental delays. However, keep in mind also that if a child is lagging markedly in a particular area of development, specific programs and intentional play activities that focus on that area can make a positive impact.

The first six months: Listening and smiling

From the beginning, a parent can provide her newborn with the perfect environment for linguistic growth. Actually, everyone who sees the child on a regular basis is a critical aspect of her language development. If you have older children, their participation can also be educational and entertaining for your infant. The siblings may use silly sentences, say funny made-up words, and sing songs that will be hilarious to your baby. An infant should hear approximately 2,100 words per hour, in assorted sentences with varied parts of speech. That may sound like a lot, but a typical five-minute conversation is at least a few hundred words. Just talk naturally, and your baby will hear the recommended number of words most hours.

The benefits of hearing words in varied sentences are astronomical. Kids whose parents chat with them on a regular basis learn twice as many words as kids who are not spoken to. Hearing plenty of language also raises performance on IQ tests and increases children's reading and writing ability when they are school age. For some parents this may come naturally, while for others it can be more of a struggle.

You can affect language and cognitive development right away, as long as you know what you're looking for. At birth, a newborn cries (while using her other signals!) because that's one of her only ways of communicating with her caregivers. She cries when she's upset, needs or wants something, or is stressed. Her cries may be slightly different for each need or want, and within a few weeks you'll be able to tell what she's asking for. When her parent responds to her cries, she learns that when she needs something, if she makes a vocal sound, her needs will be met. Quick response to a crying infant is the first step in creating the bond that will allow her to feel safe and comfortable enough to begin experimenting with other vocalizations.

After a few weeks, just when you're exhausted and completely sleep-deprived, your baby smiles at you! You're overjoyed and delighted, but your baby is realizing that smiles are what people do when they want responses, and she's smiling because she wants validation and to be part of the communicating world. Of course, we're super enthusiastic when we see our baby smile. She reacts to this response and smiles again.

A Tip from Sarahlynne

Chatting with Your Infant

- **Be a talk show host.** While you prepare a meal, place your infant in a seat near you, and tell her the steps of the process.
- **Address her during dressing.** When you put on her clothes, explain each step.
- **Chat while you work.** When you carry her around to do chores, explain what's happening, and include your opinions! "Laundry is my least favorite chore. I feel like I'm always washing towels! Do you know how many ways there are to fold a towel?"
- **Narrate your outings.** In your car, tell her where you're going and what you will do when you get there.
- **Tell her what you did after a simple gesture.** For example, after giving her a kiss, look at her and say, "I kissed you!"
- **Pause naturally in your conversation.** Pause where she would respond if she were talking back to you. This rhythm will help set the cadence of conversation in her mind.
- **Show you're aware of her.** If you are not sure what to say to her, just say, "Hello!" or "What are you doing?" If she smiles or coos back, keep the conversation going. She's trying to have a chat with you.

And soon after she masters smiling, she will begin to giggle and laugh. Your baby is learning that she has other tools she can use to elicit positive responses.

Six to twelve months: Babbling

Between 6 and 12 months, your baby begins to babble. She'll experiment with vowel sounds, such as "oohs" and "aahs," and will choose a few consonant sounds to repeat constantly, such as "da-da-da-da" or "ba-ba-ba-ba." She'll chat to herself in her crib, in her car seat, and to you. Encourage her by talking back, but pause in between her vocalizations and yours so she learns the flow of conversation. She can now distinguish between different syllables, which will soon allow her to break a long sentence into words. This conceptualization will help her to understand what you're saying much more clearly.

Between six and twelve months, your baby begins to babble. Encourage her by talking back.

By seven and a half months, she'll have learned when one word ends and another begins. To encourage this skill, make sure she can see your lips move when you speak, which will help her decode your speech. If she isn't looking at you, she won't be able to understand the words you are speaking; instead, it will sound like one long word, strung together by the rhythm of your voice.

At this stage of language development, researchers suggest playing peekaboo and giving your baby simple commands such as, "Come here," and asking him questions such as, "Do you want more?" Point to objects and tell her what they are, using repetition for emphasis. "Do you see that truck? There it is! A big truck! Truck." Be sure to include emotions in your questions. "Did that story make you happy or sad? You're happy? Great!" Of course, your baby may not respond. Or she may just answer you with "ba-ba-ba!" But she's listening, taking in everything, and learning how to converse with you. And when she babbles back, she truly believes she's saying something, so respond as if you completely understand her. Or just repeat her sounds back to her. She'll love that and will most likely want to repeat this game over and over again.

Twelve to eighteen months: Speaking a little

By 18 months old, your baby will have a *productive vocabulary* of about 10 to 20 words. A productive vocabulary is the number of words your child feels comfortable using in her speech. Her attempts at two- or three-word phrases may come out as one long word, but she'll be trying to copy the patterns of the language she's been hearing for months.

This is a great time to begin repeating patterned phrases that your child will hear in daily life, such as "hi," "bye," "please," and "thank you." This way, she can learn when ritualistic language is most important.

At this stage, your baby may be able to point to certain objects when asked. She can follow simple commands, point to her body parts, and shake her head "no." (What fun for a parent when a baby learns to say "no!") Encourage this phase by continuing to respond to her, signing to her, and praising her when she follows your directions. And repeat, repeat, repeat. When she learns something, she'll love to show it off. So ask her often, "Where is your nose? Where is my nose?" She'll delight in your enthusiasm every time she gets it right.

Eighteen months to two years: Vocabulary jump

By the time she's at the next stage, 18 to 24 months, her vocabulary will soar. Most likely, she'll be able to say two- or three-syllable words and two- to three-word phrases. Children this age can learn up to 63 new words each week. She'll copy everything she hears, from you, siblings, and other caregivers. She'll also begin to conceptualize the idea behind words she hears only once. For example, we noticed that our son was trying to put something in his pocket, just like his dad always does. My husband said, "Put the Chapstick in your pocket," and showed him how to open his pocket. Our son hadn't ever heard the word "pocket" before, but he quickly repeated, "Pocket!" and helped his dad put the Chapstick inside.

As your baby grows into a toddler, encourage that language explosion by keeping the language flowing. Continue to talk to her all day, pointing things out and responding in complete sentences when she tries to respond. For example, if she says, "Go out!" you can say, "You would like to go outside?" She'll repeat everything you say, even if it's not grammatically correct. For example, we used to say, "I'll carry you," to my son when he got tired of walking. So at 27 months, he was saying, "I'll carry you!" when he wanted us to pick him up. I guess we could have started by saying, "Carry me," so he would copy that. However, later, by hearing us repeating, "Carry me, please," to him, when he said, "I'll carry you!" he began to learn the idea behind pronouns.

Continue to emphasize eye contact and get down to your toddler's level so she can see your mouth as you speak. This will help her understand the specific sounds and syllables of each word. Use adverbs and adjectives in your daily conversation as well. For example, "Yesterday, we went to the store," or "The garbage truck is loud!" or "This food is hot! Let's blow on it." Talk about feelings, such as angry, sad, scared, and happy. Show her signs in the community, such as "Stop" or "Walk," and explain what those directions mean. When you see a word like "stop," playfully remind her that the word "stop" also sounds like "hop" and "pop." Additionally, ask questions like, "What does the cat say?" and choose different animals to help her practice new sounds with her mouth. By repeating animal sounds, she's using varying lip, tongue, and mouth movements and becoming comfortable with what her mouth can do, practicing for words and flowing sentences. For example, "buzz," "meow," and "quack" all use different tongue and lip movements and vibrations, readying her mouth for more advanced language.

Repeatedly ask your toddler the same questions and help her answer them so that she understands what you mean. For example, "What was one activity that we did today?" Give her about 30 seconds to respond, and if she doesn't answer, remind her of a few of the activities you did that day. Learning concepts such as "today and yesterday" is difficult, and it will take time for her to learn appropriate answers.

She may mispronounce words, be grammatically incorrect, have trouble following directions, or even just stare at you when you give her a small task or invite her to repeat a new sound. Don't correct her; rather, model correct pronunciation, slow down, and repeat yourself. Cheer her on when she correctly pronounces difficult words or follows your direction. In fact, until she's about 18 months old, she can't even understand nouns when they're located in the middle of the sentence. There are just too many words strung together, and she'll become easily confused if she can't pick out the basic idea of what you're saying.

Fortunately, most sentences spoken by parents begin with common words, such as "I," "who," "let's," "would," "what," "that," or "this," so for toddlers, only part of each sentence is new. She understands what part of what she hears means, but will have difficulty with new words, searching for their meaning based on their placement in the sentence. Parents can combat this by repeating the same thought in as many variations as possible. For example, "Put the doll in the box. The doll goes in here. Put it in the box. Great! The doll is in the box!" When a parent does this, the child hears the repeated word, "doll," and associates it with the word "it," which was used as a substitute for doll. The child also heard the word "doll" three times, and each time, the word "doll" was in a different place in the sentence. The parent should also use gestures with this exercise, picking up the doll, showing the child the box, and even modeling the behavior if necessary.

Two to three years: Grammar spurt

A few months after my son's second birthday, he started to ask, "What's that?" all day long. His questions ranged from asking about a car beeping to the sound of a hammer to the very familiar sound of the washing machine. But he wanted more than an answer; he wanted a word to go with the sounds he was hearing. So we answered his questions, over and over again, even though he asked about the same sounds each day.

Two to three is a year of gaining physical and emotional independence. Your child will experiment with "no" when you ask her to do something, interrupt you when you talk, or even repeat every single word you say, just to get the feel of those words on her tongue. She may reenact a story as you tell it at dinner, or ask for your attention as soon as you start talking to someone else. She may "read" her books, and you'll be startled at her accuracy with the words. She may repeat song lyrics, quote television shows, or repeat rhymes from books during her imaginary play.

At this point, she's not only picking up on the words but also noticing the nuances of conversation. She's seeing that the pauses she noticed as an infant actually mean something in conversation, that some people use gestures to speak, and that inflection is important in questions and exclamations. This is also a great time to introduce manners. When your child requests, "Milk!" you can say, "Milk, please?" and she will eventually copy what you model.

If parents (and other family members!) talk to their babies frequently, use parentese, and respond to their babies' efforts at language, their children will have conquered most of the basic rules of grammar by the age of two. Long-term studies that trained parents to do so showed that by the time their children entered high school, 62% of them were enrolled in gifted or accelerated programs.

By the time your baby turns three, she'll have had what researchers call the *grammar spurt*. She can now speak in complete sentences and will begin asking more "why" and "how" questions. Get ready to answer questions about everything! She may imagine her own world while playing (this will happen even earlier for some children) and will verbalize this world as she creates it. She'll also become incredibly interested in the world around her and how it works. An endless series of "Why is the . . . " and "How does a . . . " will occupy many of your conversations with your toddler. Although being a human encyclopedia can be exhausting, answer all her questions as best you can. This pattern encourages curiosity and teaches her that language is a healthy way to converse with others and find out new information.

This is also the time when your baby will socially start to understand the effects of her words and behaviors on others. At this point, she may start to learn to curb her impulses and outbursts, if she hasn't done so already. For example, if your toddler tells her older sister, "No, mine!" when she's holding her toy, and for months you've been trying to explain why this is inappropriate behavior, she may finally start to understand how these words make her sister feel. She may also be able to understand an alternative to "mine," like, "Can I have my toy back in a minute?" She'll be able to express her emotions to you as well; a very welcome change for the parent who's been trying to understand her child's needs for almost three years.

Helping Your Child Develop Stronger Language Skills

I love having little chats with my two-month-old. Whenever I talk to her, she kicks her legs and moves her arms in excitement but keeps her eyes focused on my face. She may not be talking back to me with words, but she is reacting! She's having a conversation with me. And because I react back to her, she continues her movements and sometimes I get to hear her little vocalizations, too! As it turns out, her reaction is backed by research.

Rhythmic coupling

Reacting to your infant's language cues can actually be more important than talking to her. Parenting researchers Michael Goldstein and Jennifer Schwade studied *rhythmic coupling*, a term explaining how parents and babies "take turns" talking. In this groundbreaking study, a mother and her nine-month-old baby interacted in an observation room. The mother wore an earpiece and was asked to respond to her baby in a nurturing, physical way when she heard the words "go ahead." For the first 10 minutes, the two played together without intervention. However, after the first 10 minutes, the researchers said, "Go ahead" to the mother, and when she heard this, she reached out and touched her child in a nurturing way. The mother didn't know why she was being told to "go ahead," but she followed instructions anyway. However, the researchers were testing the benefits of her reaction to her baby's vocalizations. Every time the baby made a language sound, the mother was told to "go ahead" and touch her child.

The results were stunning. During the first 10 minutes, when there was no physical, nurturing intervention to the baby's vocalizations, the participating babies made an average of 25 vocal sounds. But once the mother was reacting to every single effort in a physical and nurturing way, the baby vocalized about 55 times! And the sounds became more complex as well. The babies made almost all the vowel sounds and became clearer with their efforts at consonant sounds. The babies were actually "speaking" as if they were five months older than they were!

These researchers learned that the high number of times parents reacted to their baby's efforts at communication directly correlated to their children's efforts at vocalizing more, and consequently resulted in quicker and more advanced language development. The babies may have felt validated by their mother's touch when they vocalized a sound and, eager to please, tried again. Motivated by this attention, they may have begun to listen to her more closely, watching her lips move and studying her face, trying to copy her as much as possible.

As adults, we all hope for attention, for someone to be listening and reacting to what we are saying. This study illustrates that babies are no different! They may not be speaking in sentences and full thoughts, but they're vocalizing just the same. By being reacted to in a positive and physical way, they're learning that communication is a positive interaction, one that feels cozy and happy.

Quantity and variety of words

Strong research has indicated that a larger quantity and wider variety of words heard by a young child can contribute to more advanced language skills later on. A longitudinal study examined 42 children from three months to three years old. The researchers visited the children in their homes once a month, recording each verbal interaction to the baby and from the baby. Over this period of a few years, they noted extreme differences in the children's language environment. Whereas some children heard many words, others heard very few. Most children heard a similar amount of "business talk," but only some were given the opportunity for a lot of additional, conversational chatting. By age three, the "children who had heard 33 million words with 500,000 affirmations had Stanford–Binet IQ scores approximately 25 points higher than those of the children who had heard only 10 million words and fewer than 60,000 affirmations. . . . Children's scores on vocabulary, language, and academic tests at age 9 years correlated strongly with their vocabulary use at 3 years and even more strongly with the language input they had received from their parents in those early years."

This study, which has been replicated in many others, affirmed the theory that if a child, in her very early years, hears a larger amount of words with strong variety, then she will score higher on IQ performance tests, and these results will last into later childhood, as shown by the scores at age nine. The researchers mention "affirmations." What does that mean? When you affirm your infant and toddler's efforts at language, you practice rhythmic coupling and respond to them with facial expressions, gestures, words, and conversation skills.

Your baby's language cues

You can recognize your baby's early language cues in the form of vowel and consonant sounds. But how do you know if your baby is making a language sound rather than a "baby" sound? Hint: Coughs and grunts are not vocalizations! See the sidebar for some signs you can look for.

When you respond to your baby, speak to her as if you're having a conversation. Allow appropriate amounts of silence to go by (just like you would in regular conversation) before you react. If you're at a loss for words, you can try, "Is that true? Did that make you happy or sad? Wow, really?"

A Tip from Sarahlynne

Recognizing Your Baby's Language Sounds

- **Listen for long, drawn-out vowel sounds.** Your baby makes sounds, such as "aah" or "ooh."
- **Watch for her first consonant sound.** This may be ***/d/***, one of the first sounds a baby's mouth muscles can form.
- **Notice if she is "cooing."** Cooing is one of those things that's impossible to describe but so incredibly obvious to parents when their baby does it.
- **Be ready for combinations.** An older infant will say consonants and vowels together such as "da-da-da-da" or "ba-ba-ba-ba."

Speak to your baby as if she were a friend. Use her cues to react appropriately. But please, don't put too much pressure on yourself! If you're aware of the benefits of reacting to her language efforts, you'll be more in tune with her needs as she develops her communication skills.

Of course, the early stages of language development can be frustrating. You can't always tell what your baby wants, but often your baby knows exactly what she wants; she just can't tell you. She may be hungry, tired, bored, or uncomfortable, or she may need a diaper change. You try everything trying to figure it out, and often her frustration escalates to a very high-pitched wail before you realize what she needs.

But there is a solution. Enter sign language.

The Benefits of Sign Language

Sign language is an excellent tool for encouraging your baby to communicate with you before she's ready to speak. It cuts down on frustration and shows you that she's indeed listening and responding to you! Even though you'll be verbally reacting to her coos and sounds, using sign language is another way to give her the opportunity to begin two-way communication.

Teaching your baby to sign also can have cognitive benefits. Research has shown that sign language helps babies acquire speech earlier, increases their vocabulary, and increases their IQ scores and brain development. Signing activates a part of the right side of the brain that's connected to visual-spatial processing and helps it to develop more fully than if a child is only spoken to. Consequently, children who learn some baby signs become excellent multisensory learners and can pick up on new information through visual, auditory, and kinesthetic stimulation better than children who don't. That is, you're giving your child a multisensory experience when you sign to her. She hears the word, sees the word form on your lips, and is given a movement to match the word.

Connecting movements with verbal gestures is so effective that when I was teaching sixth grade, we used it quite often when teaching abstract literacy concepts such as plot, conflict, rising action, and even denouement (falling action). I showed my students full-body movements that matched each definition and practiced them daily through games like "Simon says." I remember watching my students perform these movements automatically, months later, as they explained the definition, as if their muscles were helping them remember what they needed to say. Additionally, when I was teaching reading to students who suffered from dyslexia, I would always (on the recommendation of the Dyslexia Institute of Indiana) ask them to trace the letter in sand and in the air while they repeated the name and sound. Connecting movement to auditory and visual learning is key for older students and students who struggle with learning disabilities. For babies, sign language provides an excellent head start.

Sign language and verbal language are incredibly connected. Research shows that infants cannot gain a "more sophisticated vocabulary until their fine-motor finger control improves." Once a baby can sign back to you, her vocabulary will begin to soar. Because fine-motor control contributes to higher signing vocabulary, the more your baby uses her hands, the stronger her vocabulary will become.

When to introduce sign language

You can begin signing to your baby as soon as you can hold her eye contact, which starts somewhere between four and six months. The first sign that most parents teach their babies, unknowingly, is good-bye. When you show your baby that it's appropriate to wave at people while you leave them, you're connecting a movement with a verbal gesture.

When your baby realizes that she can wave good-bye and that it is an appropriate mannerism, she's now figured out that she can communicate with the world using more than her voice! And people react! What person hasn't gushed when a baby waves at them?

While you're introducing waving, you can start using other signs. The key is to always say what you mean when you sign the word. You must be consistent and try to do it every time so your child learns the movement with the word. Start with some very basic, often-used words, such as "more," "milk," and "all done."

More: Close your fingers against your thumbs and touch and separate your hands, touching the fingers of each hand gently each time.

Milk: Close and open your fists, keeping them in a vertical position.

All done: Open your hands and fingers and move them from palms up to palms down.

I started using these three basic signs with my son at six months, and now even at age two and a half, he still uses "all done" along with the actual words when he's feeling very emotional about something and needs to communicate it immediately. But initially, it took a long time for him to reciprocate these signs; often it can take between three and four months. Once he started using them, he used them all the time. He was able to tell me that he wanted more food, that he wanted milk, or that he was all done—with his meal or with his nap! Later, we added "eat," "diaper change," and "hot."

Eat: Touch fingers to thumb and touch mouth.

Diaper: Put your hands at waist height. Tap your index and middle fingers against your thumb. (This is the sign for diaper, but it can be used for "diaper change.")

Hot: Curl your fingers into a crawl shape. Pull your hand quickly from your mouth down.

I have a friend who taught her daughter a sign to go with almost every new word she learned. Whereas I stopped with these basic ones, my friend's daughter signed things like "flower," "dog," and "elephant." This little girl talks now, but before she spoke, she signed to her mother every time she saw an object she wanted to discuss. My friend would say, "Yes, flower!" and sign it back to her. She and I were constantly amazed at how quickly this little girl would pick up the signs and be able to use them in "conversation" with her mother. Their communication was fascinating to watch. Her mother knew her daughter was internalizing these concepts, even if she couldn't say the words. What an incredibly rewarding moment for a parent.

Signing with your baby

Because signing helps your baby express her desires, it reduces her stress in trying to communicate before she can talk. However, teaching your baby to sign can be a little tricky. It is important to respect your baby and be aware of individual differences. Here are few things to keep in mind while you are signing to your baby:

- Your child will not respond overnight. In fact, it may take months. Be patient, but be consistent.
- Don't begin signing until your baby can sustain eye contact with you for about ten seconds. Sign to her when she's looking at you, and make sure she can also see your face as you speak.
- Begin with a few basic signs. "More" and "milk" are two of the most common signs.
- Once your baby seems to understand these basic signs, add a few more. It is not necessary to wait until she can repeat the first few signs before adding more.
- Consider using ASL (American Sign Language) as opposed to a made-up sign language. However, the process should never be stressful. If a sign is too hard for your baby, it's okay to wait until a later time or substitute some easier signs.
- When your baby starts to speak, ask her to use the signs too. For example, if she points to the milk and says, "mmmm," you can say, "You want your milk?" (remember to model correct language) and show her the sign for milk. Then say, "You can show me 'milk,'" and sign it again. If she signs back, great; if not, that's okay too. Just keep modeling.

Sign language is a wonderful way to improve communication and promote brain development in your infant. One of the advantages of using basic signs is that the baby will benefit from it, even if the parents use only a few signs and stop using it after several months. However, some families have yet another chance to give their child an edge in language acquisition by teaching their children to become bilingual.

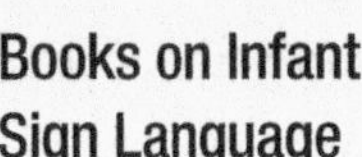

Books on Infant Sign Language

- *The Baby Signing Book* by Sara Bingham
- *Baby Sign Language Basics: Early Communication for Hearing Babies and Toddlers* by Monta Z. Briant
- *Baby Signs: How to Sign with Your Baby before Your Baby Can Talk* by Linda Acredolo and Susan Goodwyn
- *My First Signs (Baby Signing)* by Annie Kubler
- *Sign about Meal Time* by Anthony Lewis

The Bilingual Baby

Parents who speak a second language have a wonderful opportunity to teach their child to be bilingual. Don't worry if you speak only one language. Use sign language with your baby and she will reap many communication benefits! But teaching a baby a second language has incredible outcomes for cognition. Bilingual babies reap many of the same benefits as babies who use sign language. These include excellent benefits to intellectual growth and mental development, increased focus and creativity, and better problem-solving skills, says the Center for Applied Linguistics.

Imagine the head start you're giving your child if you teach her a second language from the beginning. Her brain is primed for learning in the first few years of her life, and she soaks up everything around her, so a second language won't seem as intimidating as it may later in life. Learning two languages simultaneously develops a child's ability to focus on one thing while ignoring the other. For example, my son knows "more" in English and "*mas*" in Spanish. But he also knows to say "*mas*" to his father and me, and "more" to his babysitter, whom he only sees once in a while!

Children who learn two languages are excellent at keeping track of information and will have the opportunity to communicate with others who speak an alternate language—a definite plus in today's global culture! Developmental cognitive neuroscientist Adele Diamond argues that bilingual children become so adept at switching back and forth from one set of rules to another (one language to another) that the prefrontal cortex (area of the brain that controls functions such as cognitive behavior and decision making) actually develops faster.

However, to truly raise your child in a bilingual home takes incredible persistence, commitment, and perseverance. Unlike signing, which can reap benefits in a matter of months, a bilingual child must have opportunities to practice, learn, and engage in this second language for years in order for it to be truly beneficial. It's an incredible feat, and one that's not easy to accomplish. If you're not in the position to teach a second language to your child at home but still want her to have the exposure, look for other opportunities. Perhaps a friend, relative, or babysitter is bilingual. Or perhaps you can choose a bilingual daycare. You might also take a language class to give yourself some tools.

If you already have the tools to teach your child a second language, keep these tips in mind:

- Choose one language per spouse and try to keep that as consistent as possible so as not to confuse your child.
- Speak that second language as often as possible and reinforce it with books, toys, and other materials.
- Encourage your child to speak that second language. Repeat the correct grammar when she tries to speak; don't correct her, but do model back the appropriate way to express the thought.
- Give her as many opportunities to practice as possible.
- Don't rely on DVDs to teach your child a second language. DVDs are passive learning tools (see Chapter 9) and are useless to the developing brain of a child.
- Listen to music in the other language. Songs that ask children to follow particular directions to a rhythmic beat are particularly helpful.

Bilingualism is a wonderful opportunity for some children. However, if it's not feasible for you, don't worry. There are many ways to practice language development in infants and toddlers so they are primed for strong verbal and written language throughout their lives. Parents can't do everything, nor should they! Whereas some children will learn sign language, others will learn to be bilingual, and still others will be given many opportunities to speak and respond to their caregivers. The key is to do *something*. Prime your child's brain for excellent language skills with some easy and simple activities.

Language-building Activities for Your Baby

Language development will occur naturally in your baby, but you can help her increase her vocabulary and prepare her for stronger reading and writing skills. Talk with her regularly, give her the opportunity to converse with many people, ensure that she hears a variety of vocabulary and sentence structures, respond to her cues and vocalizations, and play language games that encourage silliness, singing, and her natural enthusiasm for communication. Let it happen organically. Learning is play, and the more fun she has, the more she learns!

And here's something else. Watching your child learn to talk is probably one of the most rewarding stages she will go through as a young child. So videotape and write down all the cute mispronunciations and attempts at complete thoughts. It's absolutely delightful, and before you know it, your toddler who says things like "ni-nis" for tortellini will be speaking in perfectly clear sentences. And you'll miss the time you hugged and kissed her every time she tried to say a new word.

Activities for Ages 0–1

- **Simply talking.** When you talk to your baby, make sure she can see your mouth. A great pose for conversation is to cup your baby's head in your palms and allow her body to rest on your arms. If she cannot see you, she has no idea that you're even talking to her and will not make the strong connection she will if she can see your lips.
- **Social talk.** Make sure that she hears plenty of language. Talk to others around her, and don't be surprised if she starts babbling too!
- **Copying facial expressions and sounds.** Laugh with her and be silly. If you reinforce her vocalizations, she'll remember this positive interaction and try it again.
- **Singing.** Repetition of the words of a song will reinforce new vocabulary. Songs with movement are also entertaining for the baby and show her that movements can go with words. For example, make up songs that teach opposites, body parts, or other easy words.

(continued)

- **Narrating your day.** Remember not to put too much pressure on yourself to constantly talk. Just explain what you are about to do or where you are about to go. For example, "We're going on a play date today, and you are going to see your friend Selena! Do you remember Selena? You saw her last week at the library." Also, don't be afraid to go into the details. For example, in the bathtub, talk about what you're doing and how. "Now I'm going to wash your face! Great job. Now we wash your neck and shoulders. Does that feel soft or does it tickle?"
- **Books.** As soon as your child can focus on an object, go through picture books with her. You may not even read the books, just look through the pictures and discuss the story or just the objects. Reading books exposes your child to new vocabulary and new contexts early and often.
- **Puppet show.** Create conversations with puppets and engage your baby in the show. If you don't have puppets, socks will do just fine!

Activities for Ages 1–3

- **Listening and responding.** When your toddler says, "All done," respect her wishes. Repeat, "You are all done. Great!" Sometimes, of course, you won't be able to accommodate her wishes just that minute. So instead, respond with concrete concepts. For example, "You're all done with being in the cart? We're almost done at the store, then we will pay for our groceries, and then you can get out of the cart."
- **Leveling the field.** When you speak to your baby, remember to get down on her level. It's exhausting to kneel down a hundred times a day, but do it as often as you can. Your child will be much more receptive to you if you speak to her, not at her.
- **Expansive modeling.** Extend and expand her words. For example, when she says, "air-pane!" you say, "You see an airplane in the sky?" Don't correct her, just model the correct pronunciation, turning her word into a complete sentence. If she says, "We go'd there," repeat her sentence using the correct grammar: "Yes, we went there."
- **Yes or no questions.** Encourage speech by asking simple questions. For example, "Are you a girl?" or "Are you happy?" Repeat her answer, modeling a sentence for her.
- **Fill-in-the-blank.** We started this by accident. My son has a book that says, "Elmo zooms around the park." He fell in love with the word "zoom." After only a few reads, all we had to say was, "Elmo . . . " and pause, and he would say, "Zooms!" and dive into his pillow.
- **Telephone practice.** Give her a play telephone, a toy remote control, or even a banana. Take one for yourself, too. Have a pretend phone conversation. Practice saying "hello" and "good-bye" and ask and answer various questions that you would ask during a phone conversation. Bonus: Your child will learn phone manners while playing this game!

- **Anytime modeling.** Model what you want to happen. For example, talk to your child at mealtimes. I used to sit with my son and say, "So . . . " as he sat down to his meal. That was my way of starting a conversation. One day I got a big laugh when we sat down to eat; he looked at me and said, "So . . . " Children will repeat what they see. If you chat at mealtime or any other time, your child will see that this is appropriate behavior and will follow your lead.
- **A toddler version of "Simon says."** Give her short instructions and follow them together. "Put your hand on your tummy! Turn around! Jump!" Once she starts saying words, she can take a turn giving the instructions and you can follow her lead.
- **"I spy" on the go.** This game is so easy to play while you're in the car. Say, "I spy a blue truck!" or "I spy a tunnel!"
- **Name that object.** Line up three or four of your child's favorite objects. Let her choose one, and have her tell you two details about it. For example, "This is my ball. I like to kick it." (A younger toddler may only be able to explain her thoughts in simple words.)
- **Free reading.** Allow your child to "read" to you. She may imagine the entire story, say the words she knows, repeat one page six times, or point out the characters and say their names. Allow her some autonomy over the story.
- **Vocabulary building with books.** Give her a book with many pictures in it and allow her some time to familiarize herself with it. She can look at it in the car or while you're waiting in line. Once she's looked at it many times and become comfortable with it, look at it yourself and find one specific picture. Enthusiastically explain what you found and then ask her to look through the book to find the picture. (You may have to start by just opening the book to the page and asking her to find the picture on the page.) If she points to it, say, "Did you find the banana?" Invite her to repeat the word. Beginning alphabet books are great for this activity, because they're full of pictures in alphabetical order. Even if she doesn't attend to the fact that this has anything to do with the alphabet, she's still building vocabulary. This activity is awesome for doctor's offices and waiting rooms because it can go on as long as necessary!
- **Mock situations.** Pretend you're at a fancy restaurant while you're sharing lunch with your toddler. Talk about what you are eating and seeing at the restaurant. Or imagine she's a tour guide, and have her take you for a "tour" of the house. She can show you around, naming all the objects of the house.
- **Specific sounds.** Practice difficult sounds. For example, if your child has a tough time with the "ch" sound, give her words to practice that use that initial sound, such as "choo-choo," "chalk," and "chapel." Make it fun to practice the words by singing them or saying them in a silly voice.

Chapter Preview

- Why your baby loves to hear the same story over and over again
- How to ensure that your baby gets a strong foundation in print and language literacy
- What to do if your baby isn't interested in reading
- How to choose the right books for your baby
- Literacy activities for your baby

Chapter 5

Setting the Foundation for Strong Literacy Development

Confession: I hide books. In fact, as I write this, *The Little Engine That Could* is hiding underneath the rug in my son's room. It's not that I don't like that cute little book. I do. But it's about twenty pages, and he loves it. He loves it so much that he wants to read it five times a day. And for a few months, we did. The book is in Spanish. I don't speak Spanish, and I've memorized it. (We're raising our children bilingual.) So, as you can see, before the book went into hiding, it was well loved.

I'll take it back out in a few days, I promise. I just need a break. The fact that my son doesn't seem to need one shows that he's right on track with his literacy development. Yay, him. No, seriously: Yay.

The Benefits of Reading to Your Baby

The way that we introduce reading to our infants and toddlers has a tremendous effect on their later literacy skills. "Conventional reading and writing skills that are developed the years from birth to age five have a clear and consistently strong relationship with later conventional literacy skills," says a 2008 report by the National Early Literacy Panel. These skills include a child's ability to name letters, write his own name, acknowledge and analyze the sound each letter makes (*phonemic awareness*), and name letters, colors, and objects.

If print and written literacy are part of your day with your baby, he'll naturally begin to learn some of these skills without any formal instruction. When he gets to school, there will of course be formal training in phonemic awareness and letter recognition, but during his first three years of life, presenting literacy opportunities will help him develop a natural tendency and enjoyment of what will later become his reading and writing skills. The great thing about incorporating literacy activities into your baby's day is that since you're already making language a priority, literacy will come even more naturally. (This is just another way that all these developmental domains are connected!)

Reading to your infants and toddlers has a tremendous effect on their later literacy skills.

The value of repetition

Have you noticed that infants and toddlers want to hear the same story over and over again? Have you had that joyous experience of reading *Good Night, Moon* twenty times today? As tedious as this can be for the parent, it's absolutely wonderful for the child. The fact that he's attending to the story enough to want to hear it again means that he's gaining an understanding of the rhyme, rhythm, and singsong nature of the words. Each time he hears the same story, he connects to more of the sounds, more of the pictures, and more of the inflection.

The English language has more than 800,000 words in it. Your child is using repetition to make sure that he understands all the vocabulary and its nuances. He wants to be able to consistently use these words and concepts in his life, so he asks you to read the same story over and over again. Researchers observe, "The only way to learn the fine differences between words and to develop a broad personal vocabulary is to be surrounded by precise words used accurately." This pattern continues even as a child gets older. When I taught first grade, my students had a few favorites they wanted to read over and over again at story time. And when I taught middle school, there were kids who were so proud that they'd read *Harry Potter* six times. Repetition is learning. So, as hard as it is, try not to hide your baby's favorite books. I know, I know, I do this too. I think we all have. But the repetition is crucial for children's cognition and literacy development.

But it's not just about reading to your baby. It's also about *how* you read. Inflection, the ability to change your tone and voice as you read, is just as important for the development of fluency. And since you'll be reading to your child, you'll have this opportunity often. Inflection is so important, by the way, that pre-service teachers are actually graded on how they read stories as part of their curriculum!

If you read to your baby often and with excellent inflection, he'll be intrigued by the stories and most likely ask for lots of book time. He'll learn sounds, phonetics, letters, comprehension, inference, prediction, rhymes, and rhythms just from hearing and participating in picture books with you. In fact, babies who are read to from four months on even have a stronger receptive vocabulary (words they understand). As he becomes a toddler, he may even act out the stories, repeat them while he plays (in the same dramatic voices you used!), or pretend to read other books, experimenting with making his voice higher and lower.

Bringing print literacy to your baby

Children who are strong readers, communicators, and writers have the benefit of increased vocabulary as well as being better listeners and more creative, and they have better attention span and memory. This all starts with introducing print literacy to your infant and toddler. A study at a Rhode Island hospital tested 18-month-olds' vocabulary, splitting them into two groups: one that had been read to and one that had not. Those who had been read to frequently as infants increased their vocabulary by 40% since infanthood, while the nonreading group only increased their vocabulary by 16%.

But you can attain these benefits without formal instruction. That means you don't need to worry about flashcards or formal phonics lessons in the first three years. Human beings are wired to learn reading just by being immersed in a print environment. Phonics, spelling, and syllable instruction can be incredibly valuable for all children in terms of teaching them how to attack unfamiliar words and sentence construction, but they can come later, when these strategies can be understood and can be of the most help. Instead, immerse your baby in fun literacy activities and don't worry about exposing him to formal phonics just yet.

Most children don't need direct instruction in phonics if they're immersed in print and oral literacy. They'll figure it out when they're developmentally ready, between the ages of four and nine. The first part of elementary school is heavily devoted to literacy instruction, and every child will learn spelling and reading rules at that time. Some children will need and benefit from stronger and more formal direction in reading, especially those who struggle with reading challenges such as dyslexia.

Specifically trained literacy instructors can be extremely beneficial to a child who doesn't show natural tendencies toward independent reading by the middle to end of the developmental window.

How to read to your baby

So, if you aren't incorporating formal instruction in your days with your young child, but you want to encourage reading and writing, what can you do to ensure that your child has a good foundation for language development, reading, and writing? Read, read, read to your baby. Reading can and should happen any time during the day, but the most cozy time to do it is right before naptime and bedtime. Snuggling in a reading corner while your baby is warm in pajamas or curling up in your toddler's bed with him before naptime will help ease him into the relaxation of sleep.

There are a few things that you need to know about reading to your baby. Consider these strategies:

- Begin reading to your baby when he is four months old. Before then, your baby doesn't have the visual skill to focus on pictures or details.
- Don't be concerned with actual reading each time. Point out the colors, pictures, or faces. Flip the book over, look it at upside down, and practice opening and closing it.
- Use this time to give your baby your undivided attention. Turn off any background noise. Allow your baby to react the way he wants to during the story. He may want to stop looking at the book and nurse or cuddle. Welcome this. These reactions mean that your child is associating reading with comfort and cuddling. Perfect!
- If your baby wants to put the book in his mouth or turn the book around, allow him. Encourage him to explore however he needs to; in infancy, that usually means tasting it. If you put boundaries on how to handle a book, he may associate books with frustration instead of fun. If you're worried about destroying books, provide board books or cloth books made for this specific purpose.
- Read a few minutes at a time, throughout the day, to engage your baby. Infants and toddlers have short attention spans. Don't expect a marathon reading session. However, you might find that as your toddler grows, he wants longer reading times and can sit quietly for even as long as 30 minutes. Show him the fun in books and watch him get more and more intrigued.

- Allow him to choose the books and magazines. Especially as your child grows into toddlerhood, he'll have a few favorites. He may also choose books that seem way above his comprehension level. He may want to peruse a magazine just like you do or look through a newspaper like he's seen you do at breakfast. Even if you think, "He doesn't understand this," read the books anyway or allow him to look through the magazines. Maybe he likes the rhythm of the words, the pictures, or the tone you take when you read it. As long as the reading has an appropriate message, allow him to explore it.
- If your child chooses to engage in a different activity while you are reading, keep reading. For example, your toddler may take out his own book and "read" it while you read him his chosen selection. He's modeling your behavior and showing you that he's comfortable with his story. Alternatively, he may start playing with a toy. Allow him to do this. He will most likely, in a few minutes, come back to you to see an illustration or find out what happens next. Regardless, don't force him to come and sit with you. He's listening; he doesn't have to do it in a traditional way.

What if your baby isn't interested in reading?

Imagine this situation. You and your 10-month-old sit down to read a book. He looks interested, so you open the book and read him the first page. It's a picture of a baby's face, and it says, "The baby smiles." You happily say, "The baby smiles!" Your baby looks at the illustration, touches the page, and then closes the book and throws it on the floor. You say, "Let's look at this book! Look, the baby is smiling!" and pick up the book. Your baby starts to fuss and tries to squirm out of your arms. You say, "We're reading now. We don't throw books." Your baby looks away and works harder to get out of your arms. Relaxing with a book is now too much of an effort. You put your baby down and place the book on the couch, slightly frustrated. *I tried to read to him*, you think. *He just doesn't like it.*

This is an all-too-common scenario that can be fixed with simple solutions. First, when you're reading with your baby and he loses interest, *let him.* If he wants to read three pages and then get down and play with his trucks, no problem. You now have two choices. You can continue to read the book, modeling reading behavior, even if he isn't looking, or you can say, "You don't want to finish the story now? Okay. We can read it later." Make reading as fun and nonthreatening as possible. It's an activity that doesn't and shouldn't require boundaries.

When I was teaching sixth grade, I had a few students who participated in class from under their desks. Some would lie on the floor, and others would sit by the wall on the side of the classroom. Some were drawing pictures during my instructional time. Many teachers criticized my unorthodox practice of allowing these students to participate in class in this manner. "They're not paying attention!" I would hear. But they were. And they made better academic and behavioral strides because I allowed this minor adjustment in their learning: I didn't require their "strict focus." This is a great strategy to employ with a beginning reader. Allow your baby to nurse, play with toys, or even color while you read. The trick is to expose him to print literacy, even if he's not 100% focused on what you're doing. He'll see you and soak up your behavior. And in a few months, you may be thrilled to see your child take a book, climb up onto the sofa, and "read" it to himself. Or he may curl up with an older sibling who is reading, curious to see what's so interesting. Books are awesome and fascinating. But don't force it. Your child will see for himself soon enough.

As with all other developmental milestones, infants and toddlers will become readers at their own pace. Some babies willingly sit for a story at 12 months, whereas others will be 18 months old before they're interested in even sitting for two minutes. Don't despair. Remember that every child walks at a different time and talks at a different time. It's the same with reading.

When your child does show interest in reading, that's when you can step up your game to make reading more accessible. See the Making Reading Accessible sidebar for some techniques that can help involve your child in reading.

What to Read with Your Baby

There are thousands of children's books and even some nice kids' magazines out there. You have the options of the bookstore and library, of course, but now there are iPads, Kindles, and other screen options for reading books. Does it matter what you read to your child? Does it matter if you use electronic or paper media?

A Tip from Sarahlynne

Making Reading Accessible

- **Keep books everywhere.** Place them in the family room, in the bedroom, and even near the toilet when you're potty training! Keep a plastic book or two near the bathtub. When you go out, make sure the baby has books in his stroller or the car. Make reading a regular activity, not one that is reserved for "special times."
- **Create a cozy reading corner in his room.** Place some fluffy pillows in the corner, or an area rug. Make the space just big enough for you and him to snuggle up and read. Include some blankets and a few books.
- **If he has a favorite page, read it as many times as he wants.** My son loved a page in a Clifford book that said, "Where were his pals? They were not up! They were not down!" He always stood up when I said, "up," and fell on top of me when I said, "down." We read that page at least four times each time we read the story.
- **Encourage participation.** Make reading an active, not passive, activity. Ask your toddler to point to an object that you know he recognizes and praise him when he finds it. Ask him questions each time and slowly add one or two new vocabulary words to your requests. Pause during familiar sentences and allow him to finish the line. This works well with rhyming books, such as those by Dr. Seuss.
- **Go slower than you think you need to.** Watch your child's eyes while someone else reads to him. Most likely, his eyes will be darting around the page, trying to soak in each little detail. Don't rush him through the pages. Read the words slowly, and then when you've finished, allow him to focus on as many of the pictures as he needs to. He may even want to turn his own pages.
- **Resist the pressure to put on a show every time you read a book.** But don't speed through it. That's boring. Entertain. Make your child think that the book naming all the colors is the most fabulous book ever. You're creating a reader with everything you do. Have fun, and so will he.
- **Read in front of your child.** When your child is playing by himself, sit on the couch with a magazine or book. You may not get very far in your reading, but he will notice what you're doing and you'll be acting as a fantastic role model.

Choosing the right books

During the first few months, your infant has no idea what you're reading. Use this opportunity to expose him to the sounds of reading. I used to read selected sections of *People* magazine aloud to my son when he was about six months old. If you use fancy inflection, your child will attend to the rhythm and tone of the words. You're teaching him to pay attention to the cadence of language and how words can flow into a beautiful and relaxing melody, and that is an invaluable lesson for emergent literacy.

Once he begins to be interested in looking at pictures, find books that have high contrast in color and texture or have detailed faces, especially of children. Babies love to touch pages that are soft, crinkly, or smooth, and they love to study other faces. He'll be especially fascinated by pictures of other babies who are showing various emotions. Look for simple books with a specific focus like shapes, colors, and animals.

When your child is ready to sit for a story, consider what you want to expose him to. He'll copy the behavior he sees, even in pretend worlds. If you read him a story in which characters tease each other, be prepared for him to think this is accepted behavior. Remember that emotional negativity, not just physical violence, can create unwanted behavior in your child (we will talk more about this in Chapter 9). If you're uncomfortable with dialogue in a story, but you generally like the message, just change the words.

Books with familiar characters or objects that your child shows interest in are fun ways to bring childhood friends to life. Even if your baby doesn't watch television, he'll connect to these cuddly characters. For example, *Sesame Street* and *Clifford the Big Red Dog* have safe, G-rated characters who will entice and

Baby Book Qualities to Keep in Mind

- **Board books** (less likely to rip when he chews on them): *Good Night, Gorilla* by Peggy Rathmann; *Where's Spot?* by Eric Hill
- **Fabric books** (soft, cuddly, almost impossible to rip): *Baby's Day* by Karen Katz; *Fuzzy Bee and Friends* by Roger Priddy
- **Plastic books** (can be taken in the bath or to the beach): *One Fish, Two Fish* by Dr. Seuss; *Elmo Wants a Bath* by Joe Mathieu
- **Simple pictures with only a few words per page:** *Pat the Bunny* by Karen Kunhardt; *Tickle, Tickle* by Helen Oxenbury
- **High contrast in colors:** *Brown Bear, Brown Bear, What Do You See?* by Bill Martin, Jr.; *The Itsy-Bitsy Spider* by Iza Trapani

entertain your baby. And if your toddler is showing an interest in a particular type of toy, use this to your advantage in books! For example, if your child loves trucks, expose him to transportation books. If he loves rocket ships, read him books about space, even if they're too "advanced." Just look at the pictures and name objects.

Paper versus electronic books

I recently saw a YouTube video of a one-year-old who was playing with a book. He didn't know what to do with it. He kept pressing the "buttons," trying to change the "screen" as if it were an iPad®. While some viewers were disgusted that this baby was more familiar with an electronic device than an actual book, others viewed electronic books as a wave of the future and argued that there's no reason to keep our kids using "archaic paper books" when they could be reading from screens and saving paper.

That is something to think about. There are benefits to paper books that cannot be found on the screen. When a child has a collection of paper books, he can choose a book based on the cover, a familiar word, or a picture. He can touch each book, naming the titles and deciding which to read. Physical awareness of options gives a child a tangible understanding of the concept of "book," whereas an iPad® screen can display so many other things that the simple idea of "book" is lost among the copious options like music, games, and the Internet. "Book" becomes a part of something else, not an entity deserving its own special category.

However, a device like an iPad® offers specific benefits. For example, if you're going on a plane, instead of packing 10 books, download 10 stories on your iPad® and you instantly have a library at your fingertips. In certain situations, it's more convenient to use the technology. Just avoid using electronic books to "teach" your child technology. He'll have plenty of time later to be immersed in the ubiquitous devices available. During the first three years of life, actual books provide so much stimulation that technology is just not necessary.

And be cautious of computer programs that robotically read to your child, or books with an electronic pen that read him the word when pressed to the page. These devices take away all the comfort that reading with a caregiver can bring, replacing that cozy reading time with an electronic device that doesn't read with enthusiasm, repeat a favorite page, or snuggle up with a blanket and pillow. Reading time is bonding time, so use the electronic gadgets sparingly.

Using the Other Literacies in Your Home

Literacy is not just reading and writing. When a child becomes familiar with any situation or context enough to understand it, respond to it, and communicate within it, he is considered literate in that particular social construct. That is, literacies can include everything from being able to function on a play date (social literacy) to understanding how to handle musical instruments appropriately (musical literacy).

Family culture helps determine the literacies that a child will bring to school. A child with diverse background knowledge is likely to have an easier time in learning new concepts.

Before entering school, children learn the literacies that are available to them at home. Because each home and family is so different, all children come to school with varying schemas based on their own *situated* context, which is how educators refer to the distinct literacies that students bring to school. This is one reason that some kids easily sit and read books while others are more interested in orally sharing stories (perhaps storytelling is a major component of their family culture). It's also why some students are more comfortable with group work whereas others want to work alone. Children learn and base their new literacies on the foundations they're taught at home; the concepts and contexts they are comfortable with become the backbone of how they connect to new ideas. Literacies are ingrained from the beginning, whether you purposely place them in your child's life or not.

Think about the literacies you're teaching your baby. Are you a storytelling family? A video gaming family? A religious family? And what about personalities? Is your child around a lot of aggression? Peaceful conflict resolution? Verbal insults? Whatever he is around, positive or negative, is the literacy he will learn. For example, a family who gardens and involves their children in this activity will have young children who understand the idea behind growing fruits and vegetables. Young children copy what they see and develop concepts around the behaviors they witness. Before you know it, your baby will have become fluent in dozens of literacies. Which ones do you want to nurture in your child?

Literacy Activities for Your Baby

Talking, bonding, and communicating through the senses all set the foundation for strong literacy development. All of these developmental domains are interrelated, so in addition to the activities below, take a look at those in Chapters 2, 3, and 4 too!

Activities for Ages 0–1

- Family photo albums. Buy a fabric baby-sized photo album and fill it with pictures of friends and family. Tell your baby about each person and allow him to study the familiar faces.
- Book know-how. Every aspect of reading is new to your baby. Show him the "map" of a book by distinguishing between the cover, the pages, the words, and the illustrations. Move your fingers along the words as you read them aloud.
- Rhythm and rhyme. Find books with rhymes and strong rhythm.
- Reading in parentese. Say the words in a singsong voice.
- Practice with Cheerios. Your baby will use his "pincer" grip by pinching his forefinger and thumb together to pick up the cereal. In addition to developing his fine-motor skills and hand-eye coordination, this is great practice for later holding a pencil!

Activities for Ages 1–3

- Silly vowels. Sing "I like to eat, eat, eat, apples and bananas!" Each time you say "apples" and "bananas," change the *a* to another short or long vowel sound. So it would be "eeeples and "beeneenees," or "ooples and boonoonoos."
- Songs with movement. Sing the same songs each night before bed, and put movements with as many vocabulary words as possible. For example, if you sing "You Are My Sunshine," put your hands over your head to be the "sun" and smile and put your finger to your lips during the line, "You make me happy."

(continued)

- Finger plays and movement chants. Sing them with your baby, and when he gets older, have him do the motions for you!
    - "The Itsy-Bitsy Spider": *The Itsy-Bitsy Spider climbed up the water spout.* (Walk two fingers up the baby.) *Down came the rain and washed the spider out!* (Open your fingers and place your whole palm from his head to his toes.) *Out came the sun and dried up all the rain.* (Put your hands above your head to make a circle.) *And the Itsy-Bitsy Spider climbed up the spout again.* (Fingers climb up baby again.)
    - One of my son's favorites from our Gymboree class: "The Noble Duke of York." Place your baby on your lap for this one. *The Noble Duke of York: he had ten thousand men. He marched them up to the top of the hill.* (Slowly lift up your knees.) *And he marched them down again.* (Lower your knees.) *And when they were up, they were up!* (Lift your knees.) *And when they were down, they were down!* (Lower your knees.) *And when they were only halfway up,* (Lift halfway.) *They were neither up* (go up) *nor down.* (Go down.) *He marched them to the left.* (Bounce to the left.) *He marched them to the right.* (Bounce to the right.) *He marched them over the top of the hill.* (Hold onto your baby and lean all the way back and then come back to a seated position.) *Oh, what a silly sight!*
- Rhyming words. Say two words that rhyme. The sillier you think you sound, the funnier you will be to your child. For example, "Bunny, funny!" Say it in a silly voice and he will repeat what you say. Keep changing your voices, and watch him enjoy trying to keep up.
- Rhyming chants. Create chants like "1, 2, 3, 4, penguins wobble on the floor, 5, 6, 7, 8, snakes slither through the gate." Act out the matching movements and repeat often.
- Book treasure hunt. Lay out three to five books with a similar theme on the floor. Say something like, "I see a dog! Do you?" When your baby finds one, say, "I see another dog! Wow!" When your child gets older, make the hunt harder by adding adjectives. "I see a blue car. Do you? I see a blue bucket too!" Or encourage your child to ask you to find objects. Continue this game, making concept connections across books.
- Story endings. Close a familiar book before you finish reading the story and see if your child can tell you the ending.
- Fun words. My son loves the word *croissant.* He cracks up every single time he says it. Use diaper changes to introduce your child to words he may not hear in everyday language. Exaggerate a fun word (like croissant). Your child will be looking at you anyway, since you're changing his diaper. He may even start saying the "fun" words every time you change his diaper! Bonus: You just made a tedious chore into a literacy game!

- Alphabet flashcards. Find cards with enticing pictures, or make your own (the bigger, the better). Allow your young toddler to play with them without limits, and show him letters or name pictures. When he seems interested, start to connect each letter with its matching sound. For example, "The letter T has a train picture. *T* says */t/*!"
- Fridge alphabet. Get some large, plastic magnetic letters for the refrigerator. Your child can trace the letters with his fingers, make "words," and when he gets older, practice his spelling and reading.

Activities for Preschool Preparation

- Alphabet lily pads. Write each letter on a large piece of paper. Place the papers a foot away from each other and place some pillows on the floor as well. Give your child a letter to find. He has to jump to that letter without touching the ground, but can use the pillows and the other letters to get there.
- Matching game. Print out or draw a few pictures of objects, such as car, book, and doll. Avoid words with consonant blends, like */bl/* or */fr/*. Those are harder to hear than plain consonants. Mix three pictures with three matching letters. Help your child match the correct letter to each picture. Say "Book starts with *B!*" Don't overwhelm your toddler with choices; start with two or three pictures and letters.
- Alphabet dictionary. Have your toddler make his own dictionary by writing or tracing each letter and then cutting out pictures of words that begin with the corresponding sound or by asking you to write down words that begin with that sound. He may even write his own "story" and read it aloud to you! See Chapter 10 for a variation of this activity, which is a great sedentary project if you're feeling sick but still have to take care of your child!
- Alphabet scavenger hunt. Walk around the house singing the alphabet song. Stop at every few letters and find an object in the house that begins with that sound.
- Mailbox. Purchase a magazine subscription for him like *High Five (Highlights* for ages two through six). Involve him in taking the mail out of the box, "reading" who it's for, and opening any cards or magazines that are for him. He can even play "postal worker" with any mail you don't want. Ask him to deliver it to different "mailboxes" around the house.

(continued)

- Alliteration. Tell your child a story using as many words with one sound as possible. Exaggerate each word that begins with the chosen sound. Using alliteration will intrigue your child and make him laugh. The sillier the story, the better! For example, "Ted took ten tons of tools to a twenty-ton truck. He tried to twist the tools in the trunk but totally took all the tools out!" (Neal G., father of two)
- Letter building. Create letters with popsicle sticks, uncooked pasta (ziti works well), or Play-Doh.
- Textured handwriting. For a sensory handwriting experience, practice writing letters in shaving cream or rice.
- Playing with clay and climbing on monkey bars! What do clay and climbing have to do with reading and writing? Well, these fine-motor activities help your child gain hand and finger strength, which he will need to hold a pencil! Amazing!

Chapter Preview

- Why playtime is so beneficial
- Where, when, and how to play with your baby
- Choosing the right toys
- The benefits of play dates
- Play activities for your baby

Chapter 6

The Basics of Play: Why, Where, When, and How

When I taught first grade, I loved watching my students get lost in play. They imagined amazingly complicated situations with rules and boundaries and involved themselves in worlds I couldn't even begin to understand. Some days, when it poured outside and we were stuck inside for recess, I watched my kids spin themselves into magical worlds. They played house and pretended they were dinosaurs, soldiers, mommies, daddies, and firefighters. And when they emerged, half an hour later, it seemed they had changed.

They had grown.

They had learned.

The Positive Power of Play

Playing is a child's job. It is vital to the education and development of children. So we indulge our children in all sorts of play. Equally important, we don't over-direct our children when they're imagining their own worlds. We allow them to engage in what some development specialists refer to as *unstructured play*, a form of self-directed play with few materials and little direction from adults. This type of play has extensive benefits. The well-known education theorist L. S. Vygotsky referred to another type of play as *scaffolding*, in which the parent gives the child space to play but also steps in when necessary for safety and facilitation. Play in general, whether unstructured or scaffolded, has been shown to increase creativity, cooperation, social-emotional development, and physical well-being in the child and create bonding opportunities for parents.

Amazingly, play has also been shown to aid in developing impulse control, according to Vygotsky. When children play, they make up their own rules and then follow them, allowing for flexibility when they deem it necessary. Even if children are too young to verbalize their rules, it is evident to an observer that they've created them. For example, when my son was about two, he liked to march his animals up to his bus's door and put them inside. If I tried to join in his game by playfully putting an animal into the bus without using the door, he immediately said, "No, Mommy, no!" and put the animal back in line for the door. He'd obviously created rules for this game, and was exhibiting self-control in following them.

Fancy toys aren't usually necessary for healthy play. All a baby needs is a safe play environment, some household objects, and imagination.

A study by child development researcher Laura Berk examined how play in three- and four-year-olds can positively affect their impulse control and social skills. She examined children this age over a two-year span and learned that those who joined in complex sociodramatic play showed greater improvement in social responsibility over a period of five to six months. *Sociodramatic play* refers to creative, unstructured play that involves the children taking on roles from their lives and acting out various imaginative scenarios. For example, your toilet-learning toddler may encourage her baby doll, Keshia, to use the toilet and take the doll through the whole process. She may even ask for a sticker to put on Keshia's reward chart when Keshia has finished. Or she may feed her a bottle, pretend to nurse her, put her down for a nap, or even snuggle with her like she's seen you do with her baby brother.

The most interesting detail of Berk's study was that the results were the most noticeable in children who were seen as highly impulsive. Because sociodramatic play incorporates self-imposed rules and insists upon social skills, children who struggle with impulsivity learn that playing appropriately requires patience, listening, and cooperating with others.

In addition to curbing impulsivity, unstructured play nurtures curiosity. Researchers have argued that developing this curiosity in preschool and kindergarten is vital to facilitating mathematical and science skills in the later grades.

Creating Your Baby's Play Environment

Remember, in order for the natural benefits of play to occur, children need to be allowed to explore their worlds and games independently of adult intervention. This doesn't mean you shouldn't play with your children; it just means you should allow them to actively explore without telling them how to play. As parents, we often think we should be doing more for our children. Shouldn't we buy the newest, "best" toys? Shouldn't we show our little ones how to play with them? We have to teach our children everything else; don't we have to teach them how to play?

The answer is no. No, they don't need a ton of toys. No, we don't have to teach them how to play, and actually, we shouldn't. However, this doesn't mean we shouldn't play with them. We absolutely can and should (sometimes), as long as we keep the idea of unstructured play in mind. It's so hard for many adults to do this. For example, one afternoon my son wanted to take the clothes off his baby doll and balance his trains on the doll's belly. I was constantly fighting the urge to dress the baby. But whenever I did, he would stop me and put the doll's outfit on the floor. His game didn't make any sense to me. But it didn't matter what I thought. He was structuring his own playtime, and if I wanted to play, it had to be by his own rules.

Where to play

When your infant is young, create a space in your home that's open and preferably carpeted. If your house has hardwood floors, place a thick mat or an area rug in the room so the baby can have fun rolling around, crawling, and enjoying the play area, without the harshness of a hard floor.

When your baby is about three months old, place her on the floor with one or two toys. (Before then she'll be satisfied with just staring at your face, kicking her feet, circling her arms, and observing her daily environment.) Don't overwhelm her with too many, and do allow her to fully explore one before you introduce another. Keep these toys out for a few weeks before you rotate them. You'll know when she's finished with a toy when she stops engaging with it. Remember to let her lead, even at this young age.

As your baby grows, she'll become mobile enough to choose what she wants to play with. She'll roll, crawl, or cruise over to her desired toy. Keep enough toys out for her to have control over what she plays with, but not enough to overstimulate her.

As a toddler, she'll want to explore more of the house. She may walk, run, or jump from room to room, zooming her wheeled toys around, or sit in the hallway to have a tea party with dolls. But chances are, she'll play primarily wherever you are. Playrooms are wonderful in theory, but they often separate the child from the caregiver and so do not hold as much appeal as a room or area near the parent. Kitchens often end up being makeshift playrooms, since adults spend lots of time cooking and cleaning!

If you're like me and can't stand clutter, don't keep all your toddler's toys out at the same time. Instead, have several toys out for a month or so and then put them away for a while and replace them with "new" toys. But remember, some of the best toys are everyday household items such as spatulas, watering cans, and containers. For example, if you lay a sheet out on the kitchen floor and fill big plastic bowls with rice or oats, she

A Tip from Sarahlynne

Safe Play Environments

Play Environment for an Infant

- Provide a carpeted area or soft space on a floor.
- Keep a few toys within easy reach.
- Use pillows to help the baby sit up if she has strong head control and is learning to sit up on her own.
- Block electrical outlets, remove dangerous objects, cushion or remove sharp edges.
- Install baby gates for a rolling or crawling baby.

Play Environment for a Toddler

- Get down on your knees and see the world through her eyes. Anything at her level can be dangerous and needs to be moved or blocked. (See that crystal vase on the low shelf over there? Wouldn't that be fun to tip over?) To her, an electrical outlet looks more like a toy than the dangerous fixture that it is. (For more tips on baby-proofing, see Chapter 3.)
- Keep toys in visible bins, separated by category: all blocks together, all train tracks together. Teach your toddler to put away toys in their respective bins. For extra clarity, take a picture of each toy and place it on the bin.
- Don't have too many toys out all at once or your toddler will be overstimulated. If necessary, rotate them every few months.

can have a great time "burying" her toys, scooping out the rice or oats, or dumping and refilling the plastic bowls. See the sidebar for a few quick reminders on keeping your baby's play environment safe and enjoyable.

When to play

As we discussed in Chapter 2, some experts advise parents to set aside playtime, even if you already play with your baby on a regular basis. The formal playtime will let her know that this is her special time with you. This may help her to be more independent when you do have to cook dinner, work on the computer, or make a phone call because she's confident she'll have special time with you later.

I decided to try this theory out, to see if it actually would help my son play more independently. I instituted our focused playtime around 12:30 on most days, for about 30 minutes right before nap. Sometimes he just wanted to sit in the rocking chair with me and listen to music. Sometimes he wanted to read or play with his animals. Whatever it was, we did it. And it actually worked! Giving him this special time helped him to become more independent during the rest of the day. He knew he'd have that special playtime before nap, so if I had to answer the phone, work a little, or do laundry during parts of the morning, he was more understanding. Once my little girl joined our family, this time became even more important. Each time my daughter went down for a nap, I tried to devote about 20 minutes to playing with my son. And when it was time for his nap, I tried to put my daughter down for her nap first so I could read him his stories without interruption. It was exhausting at times, but, I believe, instrumental in my son's adjustment to his new sister.

Choose a time for focused parent–child play when you're both well rested, full, and happy. Many working parents try to play with their child after work and daycare, and although this may be the perfect time in a parent's mind, it's actually a tough few hours. Your child is tired from her day and so are you, so patience is going to be thin. Plus, there are dinner and bedtimes to contend with. Instead, try playing in the morning. The benefit of this time of day is that most kids get up very early, so you may have at least 30 minutes of playtime each morning before you have to leave for work.

If you don't have time in the morning for playtime, involve your toddler in your morning routine. While you blow-dry your hair, give her a brush and pretend it's a microphone. Give her a compact to "put on her makeup." Do a dance while you prepare breakfast, or give her a special bowl to stir so she can "help."

If you're a stay-at-home parent, choose a time that's beneficial to both you and your child. Perhaps it's after you've run or errands or done housework or after your child has napped. Don't necessarily worry about the quantity of time. It's about the quality. Your child will play all day, and you will interact with her during some of those times, but the time that you really involve yourself in her play should be planned and cherished.

Create this special time with both parents, if at all possible. If one is at work all day and the other isn't, be cognizant of creating some time for focused play with just the working parent as often as possible.

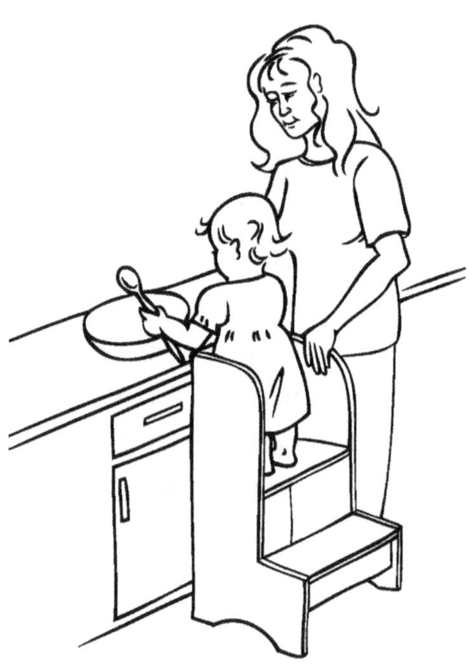

One way for busy parents to create additional time for play is to supervise their child in "helping out" in the kitchen. A kitchen helper stool with high sides should be used to safeguard against falling.

Playtime with infants is about exposing them to new experiences and connecting with them through conversation, bonding, and silliness. Take her for a walk in her carrier or stroller and point out the scenery. Or touch her legs and arms, and tell her their names. Make funny faces or sing songs. Routine times such as nursing, dressing, or changing a diaper also present a chance to play, snuggle, and bond. An older baby will love it if you build a tower and invite her to knock it down, read a book, have a "chat" at breakfast, or make a quick fort and hide out together. It's very important to follow her lead. Begin a game, and if she likes it, continue. If she doesn't, stop and try something else.

If you have an older baby or toddler or more than one child, allow the child to choose the game whenever possible. Let her pick the setting (her room, the living room, outside), and let her tell you what you're going to do. If your child has trouble choosing what to do, give her two choices. For example, "Would you like to play downstairs or upstairs?" "Would you like to play with blocks or trains?" You can start an activity, but allow her to take it in the direction she wishes. Do a puzzle, have a tea party, color, have a few pretend phone chats, or build a train track. The key is to let your child choose. Of course, as she gets older, it'll be easier for her to know what she wants. Infants love to be talked to and touched. But once a baby is crawling, she'll have some of her own ideas about how she wants to spend her time. Go with her lead and just play. This is how you accomplish the unstructured play so crucial to development.

Caution: Playtime is hard! Don't be surprised if you're exhausted, annoyed, and maybe even bored. You may think, "How hard can it be to play with my toddler for 30 minutes?" But without the distraction of another adult, your phone, or even the housework, you may find that the monotony of the game or the repetition of reading the same book 10 times is more frustrating than fun! And it's okay. It's okay to be bored, to be annoyed, and to not enjoy it right away. However, if you're distracted or grumpy, you're defeating the purpose of quality time. So if you're frustrated with your children's choice of game, try a few of these tricks:

- Allow yourself a few "I can't do that again" games. If you really find yourself detesting a certain game, ask your child to choose something else (but don't be surprised if your toddler refuses!).
- Take turns. Teach your children that they have a turn (for example, in building a tower) and then it's your turn.
- Turn on some soft music.
- Start with 15 minutes, and add a few minutes each time.

Have focused playtime right before your partner returns from work, or choose a time when there is about to be a huge transition in the daily routine, like before you go to work or eat dinner.

Once you start focused play, try not to stop until it's over. That means no rushing over to your phone if it rings or getting a glimpse of your email. During predetermined playtime, show your child that she is the priority. There will be other times in the day when she's playing independently, playing with you casually, or following you around as you do housework. Let her own the special minutes of playtime.

Encouraging "alone" time: Your children should and will spend plenty of playtime by themselves and with each other. This is just as important as your playtime with them. Playing alone will build confidence and encourage imagination. And when one child is playing alone, you can enjoy a child-directed activity with the other.

Encourage your child to play independently when she's calm and content. My son plays the best right after dinner. After he finishes eating, he goes into the family room and plays with his toys while his dad and I have a few minutes of conversation. Other children may play well in the morning, after waking from a restful night sleep, and still others may play well right after the end of a play date, when they need a few minutes of quiet downtime.

How to play

Always encourage active play. For example, ask your baby to look around, and point new objects out to her. Help your crawling or walking baby find the toy she wants by holding her hand and guiding her. Get on the floor with your active toddler, and allow her to play out her imaginative worlds. Encouraging active play will teach her that her thoughts and opinions are respected, which can contribute to greater self-esteem and more active thinking.

The way you speak during playtime is important as well. Use a child's version of the Socratic method: Restate what she says using proper grammar, validate it, and move her thoughts forward. For example:

Child, pointing to two stacked blocks: It's a tower! People climb to top.

Parent: I see the people climbing to the top! What's at the top?

Child: Treasure!

Parent: A treasure is at the top? Wow! What's in the treasure?

Child: Special treats!

Parent: Oh! Yummy treats! How are they going to carry them down the tower?

Child: In the basket!

In this situation, the parent asked one question per comment, being careful not to overwhelm his toddler with too much information. He followed his child's lead, encouraging her thoughts, no matter how irrational or silly.

The importance of "yes": Remember that when a child plays, she's often acting out an event in her life that she's trying to understand, wants to expand upon, or is afraid of, so it's important to say yes more often than no. Experts advise that parents should "say yes, follow the child's lead, set aside playtime and allow the child to push her limits, even if that means our discomfort." For example, your child may want to hop on one foot while waving her arms in the air while she walks down the street to the park. There could be lots of people around, and you're embarrassed, so you suggest a more low-key walk. Try not to do this. Even if you only participate for a few minutes, it'll make a big difference in your child's ability to enjoy play. If after playing for a few minutes you're still very uncomfortable, you can suggest an alternative. But do try to embrace the silliness and have a good time. If you join your child in acting ridiculous, you are bound to be the most popular parent on the block (with the infants and toddlers, at least!).

Of course, if your child wants to play out something dangerous or inappropriate, use your judgment on how much to allow. There have to be some boundaries for play, and safety or social inappropriateness is always a good place to draw the line. If you're feeling extremely embarrassed about your child's suggestion, it may be a good indicator that her choice of game is socially inappropriate. It's okay, and important, to teach your child this when necessary.

Cleanup strategies: When it's time to clean up, that's when you can give your child more direction. Teach her the process of putting toys away by being very clear about what she needs to do and how; for example, "Pick up your bus and put it in the basket." When she accomplishes this task, give her another simple direction. After some time, when she gets very good at listening to one-step directions, you can ask her to pick up categories of toys, such as "all the blue toys" or "all the blocks." Say it in a silly voice, sing a song, have a cleanup race, or play music to make this task more fun. Praise her each time she follows your direction, and eventually, cleaning up will become part of the usual routine for her.

If you model cleaning up, she'll copy you naturally. For example, if you always put her books on her bookshelf, don't be surprised when she does this herself! Your young child won't clean up perfectly every time you ask her to, but if it's integrated into your daily routine, hopefully the process will be easier for you and your toddler.

The Vast World of Toys

Babies are given toys from the moment they enter the world. Rattles, teddy bears, and plastic keys morph into the blocks, dolls, and trucks of toddlerhood. Before you can blink, your home is filled with toys, stuffed animals, and electronic "educational" playthings that promise higher cognitive function. We're bombarded by advertisements that tell us to buy toys for our kids and to give them every stimulating entertainment device out there, because if we do, our kids will be smarter and happier.

The opposite is actually true. The more toys a child has, the more her "inner life" could be stunted. Purchasing too many toys may teach her that objects, rather than experiences, are what create happiness. Have you ever seen an overstimulated toddler? Often, this is because she had too many choices. She was offered everything in the cupboard for lunch and now she's crying because she can't pick just *one* food. It's the same with toys. When a toddler has too many, she can't decide which to focus on, and instead she may move furiously from thing to thing, not really playing with or truly exploring anything.

My son has five toys that we call trucks. I had them all in one big basket in the living room. He usually played with his top two, his garbage truck and his bus, and left the rest at the bottom of the basket. But then I did my own experiment. I put one truck in storage, and put two upstairs in his room. The results were amazing. He played with the two upstairs whenever we were upstairs, and the other two, the ones that lived at the bottom of the basket, became his priority when he played in the family room. He began to appreciate every single one of his trucks, playing with each of them during different parts of the day.

What toys should you buy?

I have some friends who are toy minimalists and others whose houses are full of everything available for their little ones' entertainment. Purchasing a toy for your child can be an incredibly personal decision. Furthermore, our children become consumers before they can even decide what they want to play with. The toy shelves at many stores are lined with colorful plastic objects that talk and sing, toys that promise to "teach your toddler to count," and various character-themed toys that encourage a relationship with a famous childhood friend such as Elmo or Bob the Builder. It's so easy to be swept up into consumerism for our children. Between holidays, birthdays, and all the toys available in every store and online, we're constantly tempted to buy new toys.

Research has also shown that some families may feel that because they can't afford to buy certain toys, their kids won't have the right opportunities to be creative and involved in the "correct" type of play. But they should stop worrying. One study noted, "Parents who cannot afford these market-driven materials may feel disempowered to actively play with and enrich their children using the most effective tools—themselves. Children's creativity is enhanced with the most basic toys, blocks, dolls, and art supplies. Children's academic preparedness may be most developed with low-cost time spent reading with parents." It's important to remember that kids don't have to be taught to play. Children just need attention from you; a few basic items, such as blocks, dolls, or even just everyday items such as containers, pots, and wooden spoons; and a chance to use their own imagination without boundaries. And don't forget the classic key to unlock your child's imagination: books. Library cards are free, and time spent checking out books and reading will encourage your child to associate reading with love, attention, and family. So don't worry if you don't buy lots of toys for your child. A great many of them just aren't necessary.

When you do shop for toys, be careful. Not all toys are created equal. Look for toys that can be used for multiple games as well as toys that promote imagination, problem solving, and opportunities for learning cause and effect. Beware of the electronic toys. They're not as beneficial as they claim to be. According to Kim John Payne, author of *Simplicity Parenting*, these toys are too "fixed" because they are "finished." In pressing a button to operate this type of toy, your child doesn't have to use her imagination or any problem-solving skills. These toys encourage a certain direction of play, which undermines the whole idea behind unstructured and self-directed play. Instead, your child just learns to follow directions, which has its place in other aspects of childhood but in this case doesn't leave much room for imagination!

As parents, we can't listen to the marketers. Their job is to make us think we need to buy lots of toys for our young kids. We have to heed our own instincts and knowledge of optimal development for our children. Here are a few simple tips and reminders for buying toys for your child:

- Most toys should not be electronic.
- Toys should encourage imagination or problem solving (or both) and not be too "finished."
- It's okay to buy your child gender-specific toys. And it's okay to buy toys that aren't marketed to her gender.

- Notice which toys she actually plays with and put the rest away, rotating toys when she tires of the ones that are on display.

Developmentally appropriate toys

In purchasing toys, it's important to have a purpose in mind. A newborn or a young infant doesn't need any toys. She has you, and she has her environment. She'll love to look at things, especially faces, and will of course enjoy putting everything in her mouth! She may like to hold something now and then, so a rattle or baby keys will do just fine. And when she begins teething, she'll like toys that are long enough to hold and simultaneously chomp on. When she expresses interest in holding something, give her a plaything with various textures: smooth, crunchy, silky, and bumpy. I used to dangle a multitextured teething toy over my son's tummy, and when he tried to grab it, I'd move it closer or farther away, depending on his mood and level of giggles. After a few seconds, I'd have the toy give him a hug.

Tummy time is a very important part of an infant's day (see Chapter 3). Unfortunately, many infants hate it. That position can be uncomfortable for a baby who doesn't have the head or abdomen strength to pull herself up. To help her to strengthen her core and prepare for crawling, place a colorful, textured toy next to her while she rests on her stomach. Alternatively, purchase a colorful "tummy mat" that has stimulating designs for the baby to study. Later, when she can lift her head off the ground, she may actually reach for a toy. Large blocks, plush toys, trucks, and stacking toys will provide more than enough stimulation.

Once your baby begins to sit up on her own, she'll enjoy holding and letting go of objects with various textures. Give safe objects that she can discover through taste and touch, such as large plastic baby keys, kitchen "toys" such as large utensils and containers, a stuffed animal, or big plastic or wooden blocks with surprises safely built in, such as a ringing bell or a few sliding smaller blocks. Give her a few at a time, so she can turn them over, push them together, and pull them apart. Make sure to give her abdomen and back some solid support so she doesn't have to worry about balancing herself and can use both hands to play.

The next stage, crawling, is the stage of true exploration and hiding. Once your baby becomes mobile, she'll be delighted to crawl into cabinets, snuggle in tunnels, and move toys from one side of the room to another. She'll probably squirm out of your arms at every opportunity, excited to explore the world in this new way. Large cardboard boxes and pillows make awesome hideaways and obstacle courses.

As your baby learns to walk, toys that assist with walking are useful. My son received a fire truck for his first birthday that had a handle he could use for balance. He walked that truck around our neighborhood all summer as he became more confident on his feet.

By about 18 months old, your toddler will be ready for toys that encourage pretend and building as well as toys that allow her to copy you. She'll want to do everything you do, so capitalize on this when purchasing toys. One of my son's favorite toys at that age was a plastic cookie set that came with a cookie sheet, cookies that Velcro together, a spatula, and oven mitts. He carried the mitts around the room saying, "Hot, hot!" and put them on to touch the cookies, just like he saw me do. Kids this age should have more than a dozen toys, but each toy should be purposeful. Encourage imagination and keep the toys simple.

Don't overlook the classics, either. Balls, books, blocks, trains, nonelectronic cars, and dolls are long-term toys that will provide endless hours of fun. Your child will play with these toys in new ways as she grows. Unlike a toy made just for a specific age group, a ball or book will become new and exciting every few months. For example, as a young infant, your baby will touch and squeeze a ball. As an older infant, she may toss or roll it. A toddler will kick it, throw it, and even play catch with you. Commercial toys marketed specifically to infants and toddlers (you know what I'm talking about—electronic light shows, character toys that talk and sing, and so forth) are fun in specific (and short!) stages of development but can easily be the kind of toys that slowly take over your house. Your child may be extremely excited at first, but after a few weeks, she'll lose interest in that toy she just had to have, and you may find it sitting at the bottom of a basket, sad and lonely.

Between 18 months and two and a half years, your child will begin to imagine worlds and stories. She will no longer be satisfied to just hold a toy or push a truck along the floor. Now, she'll start to create elaborate storylines. She will hang astronauts out her bus window, set up her cars in traffic, and begin to find humor in ridiculous situations. For instance, whereas before she may not have understood the hilarity when you said, "This is a horse!" when clearly pointing to a duck, now she will find these jokes hysterical. She may also use everyday objects, like laundry baskets, as rocket ships or merry-go-rounds. At this point, toys that encourage story building are excellent. Action figures, animals, little dollhouses, or play kitchens are outstanding toys for this age.

The Secret of the Play Date

I love play dates; they're one of the hidden gems of early parenthood. Play dates provide an awesome opportunity for parents to socialize, but there are some cognitive benefits for children as well. Drs. Brazelton and Greenspan suggest, "Children need time to play with friends outside of formal activities four or more times a week to provide the complex processes of thinking and socializing that only such play can offer." A play date offers unstructured playtime in which kids can explore and pretend with others. Even if your toddler isn't ready to play with her friends, she'll participate next to her playmate (parallel play) and observe how he interacts with her toys. And don't underestimate your young child's happiness over a play date! Even a two-year-old will become excited when she is told her friend will be visiting, although sharing her toys may be a difficult concept for her. It also can be great to bring younger infants to a toddler play date. They observe the other children and pick up on nuances, language, and behaviors that may not be available to them in their home situation.

But here's the best secret about play dates: *They're just as much for the parents as they are for the little ones!* Play dates give moms and dads a chance to socialize while their babies interact and play. Somehow, on a play date, building a tower 20 times or rolling a ball around the room takes on a new energy when you and your child are with friends.

Find some other moms or dads whose company you enjoy, especially if you're a stay-at-home or single parent, and set up play dates once or twice a week. If you can, find a friend who can be your impromptu play date whenever you (or your child) need a new type of stimulation and none of your usual activities are working. I have a couple of friends whom I check in with almost daily. We plan a quick outing if we can, or if it's raining, we do a play date at someone's house. It's kept everyone (including me) happy many times!

Play dates also provide incredible learning opportunities. Many toddlers are capable of creating friendships at a young age, and these friendships can help create sympathy, develop negotiation and sharing skills, encourage kindness and empathy, and even prepare them for a future sibling! All children have different strengths and personalities and face distinct challenges. Playing with friends will give your child the opportunity to play with someone who sees the world through a different lens.

Children enter social situations using the sociocultural contexts they're taught in the home, and they try to navigate other children using these ideas and themes. For example, one child may react softly when a child takes a toy from her, whereas another may grab hold of the toy and yank it back. It all depends on her personality, previous experiences, and what she's been taught.

As you can see, children learn social skills at play dates. Whereas at home a parent may appease a child or redirect her attention if she's upset, a toddler friend won't do that. A friend may run away in frustration, steal a toy, cry, bite, hit, or even try to make her playmate feel better by sharing.

Toddlers on play dates will also react differently depending on how well they know their friend. If you've just introduced your child to a new friend, don't be surprised if they first engage in parallel play without directly interacting. This type of play could go on for a few minutes, for a few play dates, or even for a few months. However, they're watching and observing each other, and eventually they will interact. Be careful not to force the dialogue; your children will move their friendships along at their own pace.

Eventually, toddlers will communicate, whether it's in a positive or negative way, and that's when you may need to step in to help manage conflict. Dr. Penelope Leach advises, "Toddlers are not old enough to 'fight their own battles' or 'play fair' . . . they need protecting from each other so that neither gets hurt physically or emotionally." If you spend time teaching your child how to share and how to react when she is content or unhappy in a social situation with this new playmate, the friendship will be stronger and she'll eventually not even notice your presence, unless she really needs you.

Often, older children can provide a more peaceful setting for playing with a toddler. Their closeness in age allows them to be more understanding of a toddler's needs and frustrations. Your toddler will look up to the older child, and just as she does with adults, try to copy his behavior and gestures.

Play dates allow your child to test out her developing behaviors and learn from others in real-world situations. The benefits are endless, for both you and your child!

Play Activities for Your Baby

There are many play activities integrated throughout this book, but here is a quick overview of some fun imagination games you can play if you have a chance for quick quality time during the day. The idea is to stimulate cognitive and emotional activity while sparking imagination and silliness. Having an infant or toddler is permission to be ridiculous. Trust me, your child will find you hilarious.

Activities for Ages 0–1

- Creative bath time. By four months, your baby can be encouraged to splash around and kick the water in his infant tub. If you're feeling brave, put some washable finger paints in the bath and use the tub as a canvas.
- Mirror play. Make silly faces. I used to hold my son in the mirror and sing "I Feel Pretty" while we made faces. Yup, I know he's a boy. It was funny, though. He liked it.
- Airplane! Hold the baby over your head and gently move her from side to side. Have your baby come in for a landing, swoop her in, and give her a kiss. Alternatively, place your baby on the floor and fly around the room, opening your arms and making airplane sounds while your baby gazes at your movements (Marc D, father of two).
- Bucket play. Dump a bunch of blocks out of a bag, or fill a bucket with soft toys and empty them out.
- Song and dance. Play music from Broadway musicals and act out the songs, dancing and singing in an overdramatic fashion. Bonus: This one is great exercise!
- Noisy fun. Make noise with rattles, and clink spoons against cups.
- Little drummer. Give the baby a wooden spoon and a metal pot. Show your baby how to use the pot as a drum, or pretend to "stir" her food.
- "Where's Baby?" Put your infant in a bouncy chair. Place a blanket over her, first up to her knees, then to her waist, then to her chest. See if you can encourage her to kick it off. Once your infant gets old enough to take things off of her face, put a thin blanket up to her chin, then over her forehead and say, "Where is [your child's name]? Where is she?" You can first do this yourself and say, "Where's Mommy?" Then, when it's her turn, help her take the blanket off. Soon, she'll enjoy pulling it off herself! (Marc D., father of two)

Activities for Ages 1–3

- Silly day. This is great if you're stuck inside on a rainy day. Everything is silly. Eat food out of toy dump trucks, drink out of vases, drink blue-colored juice. (Anne D., preschool educator and grandmother)
- Magazine bits. Tear off pages of a magazine into smaller pieces. Bunch the scraps into a pile, and have your toddler jump into this "pile of leaves." Collect them back up into a bucket, dump them out, and do it again. (Tear apart the pages when your child isn't looking so she doesn't think ripping up a magazine is a good choice!)
- The sleeping game. Have everyone lie down and one person say, "1, 2, 3, sleep!" Everyone is quiet. The first person to make a sound loses. Make this game more challenging by encouraging everyone playing to make faces to try to get the other players to laugh! (Alison H., MPH, mother of three)
- Traveling. Give her a small bag or suitcase and let her pack anything she wants to take on a trip. Talk about what you'll need and where you're going. Suggest a few items and leave the rest to encourage imagination, creativity, and problem solving! (Kate Delaney Bailey, occupational therapist and mother of two)
- Desert fun. Fill a large, deep plastic container with uncooked rice, and throw in some funnels, cups, plastic pitchers and spoons, and toy animals. Move the animals through "the desert" or make it "rain" on all the spoons and cups. (Anne D., preschool educator and grandmother)
- Spaceship. Tape pieces of scrap paper under a coffee table. Climb underneath, pretend you are in a spaceship, and draw planets, stars, and clouds. Put some glow-in-the-dark stickers on the paper. Next, drape a blanket over your creation and pretend you're astronauts in a rocket ship! (Alison H., MPH, mother of three)
- "Moon food." Put squishy foods, like pudding and applesauce, into plastic bags. Pull up three corners and clip the fourth. Suck the "moon food" out of the bags. (Anne D., preschool educator and grandmother)
- Goopy fun. To make goop, start with one or two cups of cornstarch, and add water until the consistency is what you want (neither liquid nor solid). Put some little plastic bugs or plastic coins inside the mixture and invite your toddler to go digging for treasure! (Anne D., preschool educator and grandmother)

(continued)

- Pretend birthday. Celebrate your child's birthday on any day. Wrap a few knickknacks in wrapping paper and have your child unwrap her "present." Then, have her help you rewrap and try again. Declare another day as her favorite buddy's birthday. Decide what the birthday buddy (a stuffed animal) might like for presents (anything in the house the child decides on will do) and wrap them up together in tissue paper. Then gather teddy bears and dolls dressed in party hats and have some fun! (Kate Delaney Bailey, occupational therapist and mother of two)
- Toys made of toilet paper and paper towel rolls:
    - Put all rolls around the room to make a tunnel racetrack for cars and trains.
    - Have your child turn around, and when she's not looking, hide one of her cars in one of the paper roll tunnels. See if she can guess which one it is! Each time, take away a tunnel, so there are fewer and fewer each round. Or, to make the game more challenging, add a tunnel each time. (This is a great game for siblings!)
    - Play tunnel memory. Put six paper towel rolls on the ground. Choose two cars, two trains, and two trucks and place them in each of the rolls. See if your child can find the matches.

Activities for The "Nightmare" Hour

You know that time of the day when your infant or toddler is exhausted and needs you the most? That's usually in the late afternoon, when you're also exhausted and still need to cook dinner, put your babies in the bath, and perform the nighttime routines. (Oh yeah, and you'd like to have five minutes to talk to your partner, too!) Your children melt down at the drop of a hat, and you start counting down to bedtime. You find yourself getting frustrated with the situation and with your children, and maybe you're even waiting impatiently for your partner to arrive to help.

Sound familiar? This is a common situation for parents with young children, but there are ways to get through this time in the day. If all else fails, feed her some dinner or a small snack (like fresh veggies or fruit) first, so she's not cranky and hungry while you prepare dinner for the other family members. But first, try one of these strategies the next time you're faced with the "nightmare hour."

- Give your child an independent activity. This should be something that she can be proud of and then include you in when she's finished. For example, while you cook, your toddler can color a picture, play with Play-Doh, work with stickers, or do a puzzle. At the end of her independent activity, encourage her to show you her creation. Make a big deal out of what she made and how well she worked by herself. (But don't be surprised if at first your child's independence only lasts for a few minutes; keep working at it and add a few minutes each time.)
- Allow her to stand on a stool with high sides and let her "help." To make this activity safe, make sure the sides reach at least your child's shoulders. The stool should have at least three high sides to prevent falling and a few steps to ease the child to the top (see the illustration of a "kitchen helper stool" earlier in the chapter). Hand her a spoon, a bowl, and maybe even some bread dough, a potato, or some raw vegetables.
- Lay out a sheet on the kitchen floor. Set out some measuring cups, plastic pitchers, and dry food such as pasta, oatmeal, or rice. Have her measure the food and pour it in larger containers like pitchers.
- Open the special kitchen cabinet. If you've filled a kitchen cabinet with plastic containers, pots, spoons, cookie cutters, and other safe kitchenwares, allow your child to play with this cabinet just during your special cooking time. She can pretend to cook just as you do, emptying out all her goods and putting them back as you prepare the meal.
- Invite a neighbor over for a quick play date. Take turns with your neighbor. One can take the lead on playing with the kids while the other prepares dinner for her family.
- Make an assembly line. If you're making a family-friendly dinner, use an assembly line so everyone can help. For example, if you're making pizza, give one child the cheese and the other child the veggies. Show them the process and allow them to participate in as many steps as possible. Bonus: They may eat a greater variety of foods!
- Use the kitchen timer. For an older toddler, set a timer or put a picture on the refrigerator with two different colors. Tell your child that when the timer goes off, or when the color goes from yellow to green, you can play with her, but right now, you have to cook dinner. During the "yellow" time, or the time when the timer is moving, give her a puzzle or another problem-solving activity.

Chapter Preview

- Imaginative play and why it is important
- How to set the stage for successful creative play
- The benefits of arts, crafts, and music for young children
- Arts, crafts, and musical activities for your baby

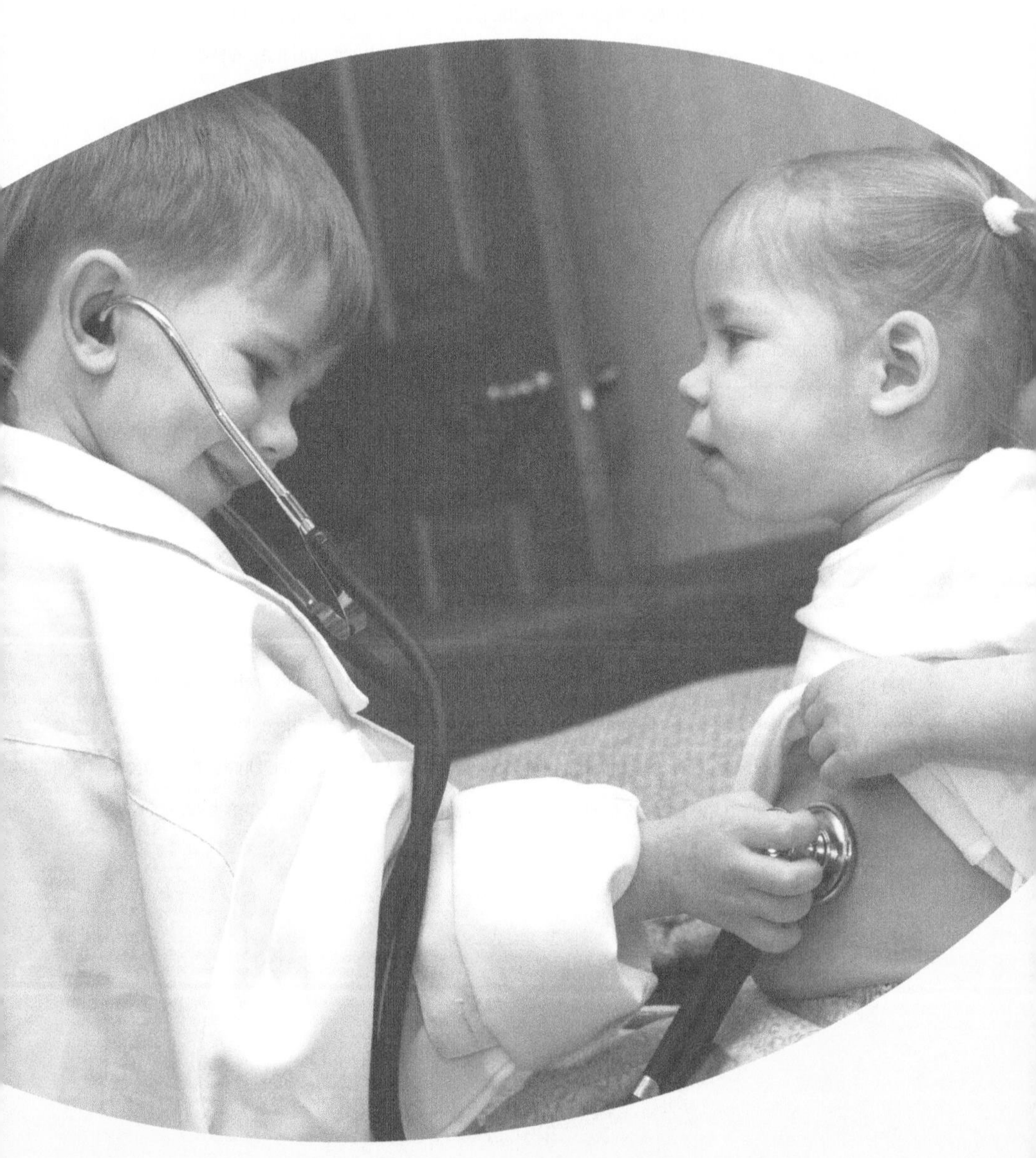

Chapter 7

Creative Play: Setting the Stage for Success

I have some friends who can create an artistic activity for their child using five random objects in their pantry. They love it when their toddler is flinging flour around the kitchen. I am so not that kind of parent. When I see flour dusting the floor, all I think of is the vacuum cleaner. Don't get me wrong; I love to play with my children. I'm just not an arts and crafts person. So this chapter is just as much for me as it is for you. But we're not going to stop with arts and crafts. We're going to talk about all sorts of creative play, from imaginative and functional play to musical activities. And we're going to focus on the second and third year of life; although you can have creative play with infants, this chapter is mainly for toddlers. These youngsters are beginning to expand their worlds, are looking for more advanced activities, and can engage in different types of play.

The Different Types of Play

Creative play is incredibly beneficial to a child's emotional, cognitive, and physical development. One of the earliest ways to foster creativity is through *imaginative play*, a form of unstructured play that has lasting benefits.

What is imaginative play?

Imaginative play is fun that is self-directed; the child's imagination creates a world and with silly rules, funny characters, and fantasy settings. This type of play doesn't focus on toys or props. They, of course, can be used, but perhaps he's changed his toys into new objects. He may have transformed kitchenwares into spacesuits. Perhaps he's holding nothing, but is running around the grass, pretending he's in a maze. When a child is playing a video game, soccer, or even a board game, he is not engaged in imaginative play. He is playing, but those games already have boundaries and leave little room for a child's own discoveries. Imaginative play allows a child a wonderful sense of autonomy; he is creating all the rules of the game. He can use all his senses as he creates a new world and will gain confidence as he tries out difficult and intimidating activities in his safe, pretend world.

Children use imaginative play to explain the details of their lives, which is why, when they ask us to join in, we should say yes when we can. Psychologist and child play expert Lawrence Cohen explains, "Playing what they want to play, how they want to play it, is our way of really listening. . . . They need us to be active participants in the play, just like listening requires active attention."

Creative arts play: When children engage together in imaginative play, they learn empathy and social awareness as they take on new roles as make-believe characters. Cognition improves as children learn cause and effect when they create situations and see what occurs as consequences of these choices. In addition to pretend play, imaginative play includes *creative arts play*, experiences with the visual arts, music, dance, and theater arts.

Imaginative play in its various forms is a basis for the concepts that children will be later taught as part of their formal education. Teachers take a student's background knowledge and use it as a springboard for unfamiliar concepts. The more diverse a student's background knowledge, the easier he will find new concepts. For example, a student who has been involved in musical activities from toddlerhood will have an easier time with math. An experienced teacher will recognize a student's talent for rhythm and use it to help him recognize the rhythms prevalent in number relationships. When you encourage imaginative play, you are creating a sociocultural context for your child; you are giving him the "literacies" that he'll pull from whenever he's faced with new concepts (see Chapter 5). The more literacies he's familiar with, the more easily he'll tackle new material, because he'll have something familiar to use as a connection between the old and new information.

How to engage in imaginative play: Playing with your child is awesome. It gives you permission to live in his world for a short time; it's an invitation to his most private lands. He trusts you enough to invite you in, and he wants to include you in the place where he feels the most comfortable and at peace: his pretend play.

The first rule of imaginative play is the same as the first rule of improvisational acting: Do not deny imagination. If your child says a block is now an elephant and the giraffe is going to drive the boat, that's awesome. Don't tell him giraffes can't drive. This giraffe can. Fantastic.

Your child's imagination will amaze you; it'll seemingly come out of nowhere, and you'll have no idea how he translated what he saw into something to pretend. It may start out small. He may hug a teddy bear like you hug him. And then he might pretend to drink out of a play cup or drive his car along the carpet. He may pretend he's an astronaut, a father, a teacher, or a firefighter.

Although play is full of silliness and fun made-up worlds, experts explain that small children also "use imaginative play and fantasy to take on their fears and create or explore a world they can master." Pretend play may be used as a way to replay frustrations, but you can help your toddler work through these feelings by being funny. Using humor, overact the part of the angry mother or the mean friend, suggests Dr. Cohen. Imaginative games give your child the chance to explore his world in a safe, nonjudgmental way, so remember to let your child lead.

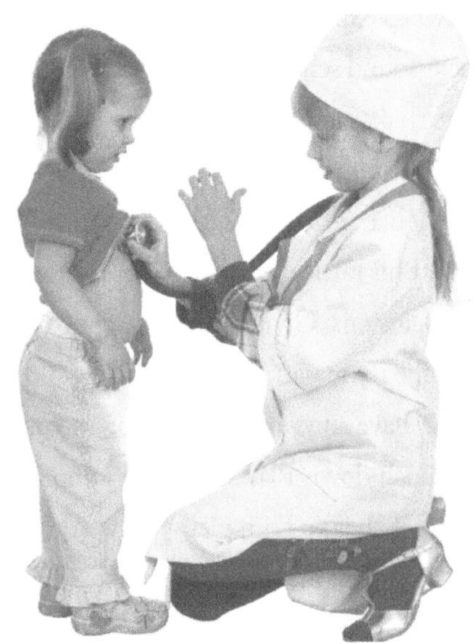

Toddlers might use imaginative play to work out feelings of anxiety associated with a stressful event, such as a visit to the doctor's office.

Your child will also use imaginative play to reduce stress, develop his *private speech* (how he talks to himself and internally solves problems), and imagine role reversals. Have you ever seen your toddler pretend to give his bear a shot? He's working out a time (the doctor's visit) in which he felt scared and powerless. Playing the role of the doctor makes him feel important. If your child responds well to imaginative games, you could even role-play this scenario before you take him to his appointment.

Functional play

Toddlerhood is also the time for learning how the world works and figuring out the things that can be expected. This is known as *functional play.* Functional play explores events that don't naturally occur. For example, a tower can be knocked down by force but not by itself, and sand is thin and slips through fingers. For the same reason, your baby throws his plate full of food on the floor or tries to drink the bathwater. He just wants to know, "What happens if I do this?" Repeating this action more than once will give him an idea of what exactly will happen next; for example, "If I throw my food on the floor, it makes a squishy sound, but then I don't get it back." As frustrating as this can be for the parent, it's important to remember that the child is working on mastering a skill, so this repetition is perfectly normal and quite important.

This skill also translates to playing with toys. A baby will eventually use *inductive inference;* that is, she will use clues from previous experiences to create a general idea about how something works (there's that background schema, from Chapter 1, again!). For example, a baby who learns that when he shakes a rattle he hears a sound may try to shake something of similar shape, like a rice box, thinking that since it is similar looking, it will have the same result. Even though a rattle and rice box may be different shapes and colors, the baby will remember what his rattle did and try it out with something else to see if he can draw generalized conclusions. Giving him the opportunity to be imaginative will help these inferences become more natural.

When children are very small, they don't have any expectations of themselves. Playing is enough. They scribble on paper, smush down Play-Doh, and jump around the room, and they are proud. They don't care if they've crumpled up the sticker and then straightened it out; they don't notice the creases in the once perfect, glossy picture. They don't notice that they haven't colored in the lines or sung on key.

Of course, our children have to be taught boundaries. They can't go around drawing on the walls or doing somersaults on the couch. But we can be careful how we frame their creativity, because we're setting the stage for how they view themselves and their expectations. For example, if your child is drawing on the refrigerator with his crayons, you want him to know that is not an appropriate use of art supplies. So you take his crayons and bring them back to his art table, explaining to him that crayons have to stay at his art table.

A Tip from Sarahlynne

Imaginative Games for Your Older Baby or Toddler

- **Create a "show" with your baby's stuffed animals.** Give each animal a personality and a special voice and be consistent with this voice and character each time you play. For example, your turtle puppet can say, in a deep voice, "I am a turtle. I move slowly." And the turtle can slowly crawl up your baby and give him a kiss.
- **Encourage your toddler to copy you in simple, safe household tasks.** He'll love to push the vacuum cleaner around the floor, "fold" laundry, put away groceries, dust, or help put plastic dishes in the dishwasher. When I used to put away my son's clothes, he would find all the socks and put them in his dedicated sock basket. He was able to do this at about 20 months. Of course, the quality of work won't be perfect, but by copying you, he's learning, gaining power over a situation, and imagining himself in your role.
- **Set the stage in toilet-training your toddler.** Give him the opportunity to train his doll first. Help your child take the doll through the entire process. Pull the doll's pants down, sit it on the toilet, wait a few seconds, make a "peeing sound," then wipe the doll, flush the toilet, re-dress the doll, and praise it for using the toilet. This may be the first step in encouraging your child to use the toilet himself!
- **Give him a doll to take care of.** When you have a new baby in the house, your older child can bathe, change, snuggle, and even pretend to nurse the doll or give it a bottle.
- **Act out situations that may be scary or difficult for your child.** For example, if your child is having difficulty sharing, help him make up a story in which two toys are not sharing and one is getting angry. Have your toddler figure out a way to work out the problem (by sharing!).
- **Create scenarios without using props.** These may include cooking, cleaning, getting a bath, taking a pet to the vet, and so forth. Go through the whole process. (This is a great one when your little one is stuck in a stroller or you're in a waiting room at a doctor's office!)
- **Fill up the bathroom sink with soap bubbles.** Let him explore the soapy texture, watch the bubbles float in the air, and squish them into the sink (functional play!). He may even put the bubbles on his face so he can pretend to "shave" like he may have seen his dad do (imaginative play!).

Don't be surprised if your child seamlessly moves from one type of play to another. He may start playing with a toy the way it's meant to be played with, and change its role to something completely surprising within minutes. He may then put his imagination to work on an art project. Your toddler is just playing; he has no idea that what he's doing is so critical to his development.

Remember, it's important to let your child take the lead in imaginative play. However, if your toddler is asking you to create the game, or you just can't play "frogs jumping on lily pads" one more time, the sidebar above offers more ideas. And do check back in Chapter 6 for other fantastic imaginative activities!

Arts and Crafts Play

Aaah, permission to get dirty. Fun times for the kids; freak-out time for some parents. We're the ones who have to do most or all of the cleanup!

However, making time for arts and crafts is a very critical piece of child development. Your child is born with abilities to be creative, the desire to explore, and the ability to exert self-control. Just as kids need to move to expend energy and expand their physical boundaries, time for art slows their brain down. As experts explain, "The creative process involves a letting-go of conscious thoughts and ideas, and such opportunities for artistic release during the day help a child surrender into sleep." Yup, artistic play can actually help your child go to sleep better!

So how can you accomplish this? Make art an everyday part of your child's life. Set up a space that is all his and invites imagination with craft supplies. Include paper, crayons, and stickers, and when he gets older, perhaps colored pencils, glitter, fabric, and glue. Keep some things, like Play-Doh, paint, and scissors, out of reach until you can sit with him, but do give him a chance to be independently creative whenever possible. Giving him one small area where he can create art freely, and then consistently directing him and his art supplies to that one area, will teach him that although crayons and paints have to stay in one spot, if he is in the right place, he can be as creative as he wants. Whenever possible, sit with him and create art to help him associate warmth and coziness with this art space.

When we think of arts and crafts, we may think of formal activities such as coloring, painting, and playing with clay. But to your baby or toddler, anytime he gets to play with a new texture, he is working on art. To our children, art is everywhere. We just have to give them the time to explore it. When your child reaches a stage at which he can follow simple directions (late toddlerhood), it's a great time to start talking about colors and shapes. But in the beginning, make it about self-discovery and exploration.

Make art an everyday part of your child's life. Set up a space with craft supplies that is all hers and invites imagination.

During the first year of life, your baby is still developing his motor control, so the art and craft activities in the last half of this chapter are primarily for toddlers. Around your baby's first birthday, you might try some fun, simple ways of having him copy you. For example, get down to his level with a piece of paper and draw a big circle with a crayon. Look him in the eye, hand him the crayon, and see if he draws a circle. Beware, however, that he might try to eat the crayon! If he does this, you can redirect him to the paper or just try again another time. Eventually, this exercise can get your baby used to creating something on paper.

Playing with Music

When I was a junior in high school, my French IV class met at the same time as my jazz band rehearsals. There was only one section of French IV. There was only one section of jazz band. I'd worked so hard to get into that band after hours of practice and stressful auditions. It was my second year as one of two piano players, and my favorite part of school. My guidance counselor wanted me to make a choice. "French or jazz band," she said.

My mother wasn't happy with those options. She knew that my music classes, especially jazz band, were where I found my happiness in an otherwise tumultuous high school experience. So she appealed to the school administrators. I was then allowed to leave French once a week to attend jazz band rehearsals. The only requirement was that I had to keep my grade in both classes higher than a B+. Basically, I took two classes at the same time.

Some people may see my mother's decision as ridiculous, as "helicopter parenting," even. "It's just a music class," I've heard people say when I tell this story. "It's not even a core subject. Why bother fighting so hard?"

"Because it was music," I feel like answering. And to me, when I was in high school, there was nothing more important. And my mother knew that.

Cognitive benefits of music

Music is not just a pastime. It's a crucial part of early childhood development. Students involved in music have proven to have stronger reading and math skills. It takes patience, focus, and attention to listen to rhythms, copy movements, and eventually gain the coordination to play an instrument, read music, or sing notes.

A study completed by Katie Overy, a researcher in the psychology of music, suggests that rhythm training, because of its innate multisensory environment, may improve phonological awareness (letter-to-sound recognition) and spelling skills, especially in kids who struggle with dyslexic tendencies. Children who have poor phonological awareness often have issues with sounding out words, spelling, and fluency in reading. But children who have played with rhythm from early childhood have an easier time connecting a letter to its specific sound. Connecting letters to sounds is just like connecting a specific instrument to its sound.

In terms of math, kids who have had formal music instruction have better spatial skills than children who have not. Spatial skills are a child's ability to visualize images and shapes in his mind and are a useful tool in math, writing, and directional skills. Music requires a child to connect the concrete concepts of rhythm and notes with the abstract concept of music. Once the connections are made correctly, concepts flow beautifully, just like drawing shapes, writing an essay, or finding your way to the grocery store. Incredible!

Emotional benefits of music

Have you ever gotten home after a long day at work, turned on your iPod®, and gone for a run? Or turned on your radio as you got in the car because you were feeling stressed? Does music relax you? Calm you? Soothe you?

Music does this for our infants and toddlers, too. Rhythm is a part of an infant's life, even before he's brought into the world. He hears his mother's voice and heartbeat in the womb, and this same solid cadence puts him to sleep when he later rests on his mother's chest as a newborn. Soon, he's surrounded by sweet lullabies and tender voices. He learns that music comforts, soothes, and even excites. Songs with faster rhythms excite your baby, and as he watches you clap and sing, he may smile, laugh, or try to move his body in response. Sing songs with various beats and tones, and watch your baby react differently to each one. For example, he may relax to "Twinkle, Twinkle, Little Star" but laugh at the silliness of "Old MacDonald Had a Farm." Because music offers so many opportunities for varied emotions and movements, it's been shown to "help children learn to coordinate their movements, channel energy, express their emotions, and connect with others."

Music Classes with Parent Involvement

- **Music Together.** For children ages 0–7 but especially popular with toddlers and preschoolers. http://www.musictogether.com/
- **Kindermusik.** For children newborn to age 7. http://www.kindermusik.com/
- **Suzuki.** Depending on the teacher and the specific program, lessons can start at age two and go through adult. Some Suzuki teachers even teach baby classes. (Bonnie Brown, Suzuki instructor) http://suzukiassociation.org/

Many parents want their children to reap the benefits of musical knowledge, so they enroll their toddlers in music lessons. I can tell you, as someone who taught piano lessons for years, starting a child in formal music training at that young age does not have the benefits you might envision. Instead, focus on the variety of rhythms, sounds, and rhymes, and your infant and toddler will develop his own love of music. Like literacy, music should be an integral part of your child's day. Sing, dance, and make rhymes and rhythms whenever you feel like it.

However, this doesn't mean that certain infant and toddler music classes are not beneficial. Researchers at McMaster University discovered that infants in music classes that encourage "active listening," such as taking turns playing instruments and singing songs with their parents, showed "larger and/or earlier brain responses to musical tones, better early communication skills, were easier to soothe, and showed less distress in unfamiliar situations." Babies will benefit from music classes as long as they are informal and active and encourage parent involvement and creative, open-ended musical play.

If you choose not to enroll your toddler in a music class, you still have plenty of opportunities to encourage active play with instruments. But remember to invite unstructured play. Step back and allow your child to discover. If he wants to tap his maracas on the floor, fight your tendency to show him the correct way to play them. Join him instead. "Give him the confidence to experiment actively with instruments," says Bonnie Brown, Suzuki instructor. However, do institute some boundaries with instruments, especially those that can be easily broken. For example, my son got a toddler-sized piano for his second birthday. I'm not about to allow him to throw it across the room. But if he wants to play it with his toes, his fingers, or his action figures, I'm all for it.

If you have a musical background, you might find a natural way to integrate music into your daily routine. For example, one mother got into the habit of playing piano with her one-year-old newly adopted son. He sat for 20 minutes on her lap listening in rapt attention while she played hymns and minuets. He asked to go to the piano several times a day.

Even if you think you're not musical, try to embrace this precious time with your child. Some parents are self-conscious about singing. Perhaps they have no ear for tone, sing off key, or don't know the words to children's songs. They think their lack of musical ability makes them unfit to teach their child music, and their embarrassment often prevents them from even trying. But your child will not care. He already cherishes the sound of your voice. He'll adore the rhythms and silliness of the music, and he will not learn to sing out of tune just because you do. If a child is singing along with you and a record, he'll adjust his voice to the correct pitches, says Bonnie Brown. She also advises parents, even if they are fearful, to be enthusiastic about music. Being playful and excited about music will arouse your child and give him a passion for rhythm and rhyme.

Praise Effort, Not Outcome

When our children are creating a new game, working on an art project, or figuring out a musical instrument, they're bound to get frustrated. And often, when they complete a difficult task, we want to praise them. We find ourselves saying things like, "Wow! Great job! You're so smart!" Unfortunately, even though we think we're doing a good thing, there are better ways to praise than acknowledging intelligence. In fact, by putting the stress on your child's brainpower you actually may be doing him a disservice.

Research out of the New York City Public Schools has noted that parents who continuously tell their children how "smart" they are are actually teaching their children to underperform! Dr. Carol Dweck created a mock testing environment with fifth graders. After being given a puzzle test, one group was praised for their intelligence ("you must be really smart!") while the other was praised for their effort ("you must have really worked hard at this"). And here's where it gets interesting. When the groups were given a second test, much of the group praised for intelligence chose the easier test, while much of the group praised for effort chose the harder test. And it didn't stop there. When the groups were then given a much harder puzzle, the groups praised for effort tried and tried to succeed, even remarking, "This is my favorite test!" However, the groups praised for intelligence assumed they couldn't complete the test because they were not smart enough. Finally, Dweck ended the study by giving each group the same test they took first. The group praised for effort did 30% better. The group praised for intelligence performed 20% worse.

What can we learn from this study? Kids who are consistently praised for intelligence will think that success is out of their control. However, kids who are praised for effort will learn that success is within their reach, based on the amount of effort they put into a task. Dweck followed up her research and learned further detail about this phenomenon. Kids who are told they are "smart" even begin to forget about prioritizing effort! Their reasoning is, "Because I am smart, I don't have to try." Or, even worse, "Putting in effort means I'm not smart enough to do it on my own, so I shouldn't have to try hard." Then, the thinking continues, "If I can't do it, it's because I'm stupid. There's nothing I can do."

We all want our kids to have high self-esteem. We may slip and exclaim quickly, "You're so smart! Great job!" But instead, we should be highlighting the importance of effort: "Excellent effort! You worked hard and you did a great job painting that picture!" Your child, even if he's a perfectionist, will have a hard time arguing with you. If he's colored a picture and there are some scribbles outside of the lines, but you say, "Great effort!" he will focus on the parts he did well, not the things that could be construed as "mistakes" (which of course aren't mistakes at all). What we're teaching our children is that intelligence is in within their control; it's a variable that is not just genetic but also requires hard work and effort.

Keep in mind, however, that your child will most likely have a strong talent for something, whether it's sports, music, theater, or reading. When you discover a talent your child has, it's okay to let him know that he's quite good at kicking a ball or has a way with words. Let him know what his skills are, just as you may acknowledge things that don't come so easily to him, so that he learns about his own talents and challenges.

If praising effort doesn't come naturally to you, don't be concerned. Just *be specific in your praise*, and *be sincere.* Try not to praise too often. For example, if your child is expected to say "please" and "thank you," it's an expected behavior and doesn't necessarily call for praise. However, if your child accomplishes something he's been trying to do for a while (like taking his pajamas off all by himself!), that's a great moment for lots of clapping, praise, and excitement.

So what does praise have to do with creative play? Everything. When your toddler is working on an art project, trying to master the maracas or kazoo, or trying to put his hand inside a puppet, he's trying to figure out a new skill, and it's frustrating. He is going to have to try over and over again before he does it right. So, by praising his effort, you're nurturing in your child a good attitude toward tasks that are initially hard. When he hears you praise him, even when he fails, he learns that the more he tries, the more pride he earns, in himself and from you. Then, when he finally succeeds, he knows it's because of what *he* did, not because of a trait (intelligence) that he was born with.

Remember, it's the process, not the product. Your baby is loving the journey, so try to slow down and enjoy it with him.

Arts and Crafts for Your Toddler

Most of these activities require a certain amount of motor control, which isn't yet developed in infanthood.

- Bathtub painting. Take finger paints in the bathtub, and watch your child paint the bathtub, the water, and himself!
- Collages. Cut out pictures of things your child loves, such as trucks or flowers. Show him how to glue them on to the paper. He can help you look for the pictures, too!

- Hearts and crafts. Encourage him to decorate any birthday or Valentine cards he gives his friends. You can cut out the hearts or just fold a piece of paper in half and write the message, and he can affix his favorite stickers.
- Sponge painting. Hang a paper from clothespins. Dip a sponge in a little paint on a paper plate and show your child how to gently tap the page to create color.
- Painting with unexpected tools. How does it feel to paint with bubble wrap? What kinds of shapes show up on the paper? How is that different from the texture of a toothbrush? A sponge? A marshmallow? (Dawn D., mother of two)
- Tissue paper collage. Cut out small pieces of tissue paper and invite your child to glue the colorful papers onto a shape or piece of paper. For a younger child, mix a bit of glue with water and use a paintbrush dipped in glue to paint the tissue paper onto the shape. This can be done for holiday decorations (decorating pumpkin or snowman shapes) or just for fun. Instant stained glass! An older toddler can sort the tissue paper into colors before proceeding with the activity. (Liz Rogers, preschool educator and mother of two)
- Cream and glue. Mix shaving cream and glue together to make a soft, liquid substance. Use this fun texture to make snowmen on construction paper. (Dawn D., mother of two)
- Shaping up. Cut out colored shapes or buy precut sticky shapes. Make simple patterns on construction paper. Say, "Heart, circle, heart, circle . . . what comes next?"
- Name that shape. Put two different shapes in front of your toddler and ask him to find the one you ask for: "Which one is the square?" Then, add one more.
- Freewheeling. Take vehicles of all types and sizes and run the wheels through tempera paint. Drive them over a big piece of white paper to see new patterns and colors. When finished, give the cars a "car wash" in a bucket of water. (Liz Rogers, preschool educator and mother of two)
- Toys in a row. Line up seven or eight familiar toys. Identify them by name and color and have your child pick them out of the line. For example, say, "The truck is blue," and see if he chooses the truck. After he's able to do that, start asking questions like, "Which one is the blue toy?" or "Which toy has purple and green in it?"
- First sketchbook. Buy some decorative duct tape. With your child, wrap up a special drawing notebook for her drawings. Give her a chance to use various patterns and colors of duct tape while making the notebook her own style. (Marissa H. mother of three girls)

(continued)

- Aluminum foil. Use foil to make shapes or wrap toys. Ask your child to find the triangle, the square, or the circle. Or, once the toys are "wrapped," put them all in a row and move them around. See if your child can guess which toy is under which wrapping.
- Art therapy. Some children love to draw out their feelings. When I taught kindergarten and first grade, we had a "Peaceful Place," where students could draw a picture when they were angry or sad. An older toddler may find this activity therapeutic. After he's finished, talk about his picture and his emotions.

Musical Activities for Your Baby

As we've seen in this chapter, music appreciation can begin very early for your baby. There are activities for infants as well as toddlers.

Activities for Ages 0–1

- Daily songs or rhythms. Sing songs or speak in rhythms for daily activities. For example, "This is the way we wash, wash, wash your hands, we're going to wash your hands right now."
- Songs with funny sounds and voices. Use tunes you already know, such as "Old MacDonald Had a Farm," "The Wheels on the Bus," "Head, Shoulders, Knees, and Toes," and "Bingo." Add movements to the songs whenever possible.
- Dramatic singing. Bring your voice very low or very high and exaggerate your mouth movements. Sing about concepts that may be scary to children to make the abstract fear more accessible and not so frightening. For example, the "I Hear Thunder" song, a favorite from Gymboree: *I hear thunder, I hear thunder.* (Stomp feet on the floor.) *And do you? And do you? Pitter patter raindrops, pitter patter raindrops,* (Gently flutter fingers on the floor.) *Yes, I do! Yes, I do!*
- Creating a beat. Tap on the floor and sing rhymes to go with the beat. Put your hands on the floor and then clap them together. Continue moving from floor to clap through the rhythmic words. Use simple rhymes such as "Row, row, row your boat," the alphabet song, or counting to 10. Keeping a beat steady is the important part of this activity. When your child is old enough (probably almost two), he will join in the beat!
- Silly musical sounds. Use "ding-dong," "tap-tap," or "beep!" Onomatopoeia is a way to have fun with tone, sound, and volume.

- Musical instruments. Maracas, xylophones, tambourines, kazoos, and drums are so much fun for children this age. Alternatively, give your child a wooden spoon and various items that will make different sounds when played. Use paper towel tubes as makeshift "trumpets" and line paper cups up like drums. Shake breadcrumb tins and cereal boxes like maracas.

Activities for Ages 1–3

- Bedtime songs. Sing the same songs before bedtime each night. Don't restrict your child's movement while you sing. Some nights he may want to snuggle, but other nights he may want to dance and jump. Soon, he may start "singing" the words or even come up with his own lyrics. Once, my son sang the word "waffles" to match the entire melody of the song "You Are My Sunshine."
- Recorded music. Turn on children's music in his room while he plays. Find lyrics that encourage movement, such as "Clap your hands, stomp your feet, say 'I love you!'" Model the dance a few times, and then your child will begin to independently follow the directions in the song.
- Paper tube. Make loud and soft sounds into a hollow paper towel tube. Make one sound and have your child copy you. Make two sounds in a row, and see if he can copy you. Get progressively harder as his skill improves.
- Musical arts and crafts. Soft background music will soothe your child and create a cocoon for his imagination as he draws, colors, or paints.
- Homemade instruments. Pour rice, noodles, or Lego pieces into plastic containers and shake them to hear the sounds. Experiment with varied sizes and weights of the objects inside the containers.
- "Bang, bang." Gently bang on soft furniture, toys, driveways, or wooden tables. Talk to your child about how each texture sounds when you "bang" on it.
- Melodic word. Find a word that your child loves and say it in many musical tones. Split it up into syllables, and make one high and one low. Then do both low. Then do both high. This is a great one for a cranky child; it takes his mind off his frustrations, especially in the car or during a diaper change. (Marc D., father of two)
- ***Sound of Music*** songs. Sing "Do-Re-Me-Fa-So-La-Ti-Do," just as you would the alphabet song.
- Wearing bells. Give your child bells to wear as a bracelet or anklet, and "shake, shake" throughout the day.
- Dynamics. Practice "soft" and "loud" by banging softly and loudly, screaming loudly, and doing "silent screams" (opening mouth and pretending to scream).
- Dance. This can be done as often as the mood strikes!
- Car music. You don't have to listen to children's music while doing errands with your child. Take a tour around the world and give your child a chance to listen to eclectic beats, dissonant melodies, and unusual instruments.

Chapter Preview

- Why nature and community outings are important to a child's development
- The benefits of taking your baby outdoors
- Suggestions for taking your baby out into the community
- Nature and community activities for your baby

Chapter 8

Exploring Nature and the Community with Your Baby

Do you take your baby outside every day or almost every day? In the beginning, it's about utilizing her senses: the feel of a snowflake or the brush of wind on her face. I had a friend who took her daughter out for a walk every day, rain or shine. It wasn't a long walk, especially on cold days, but it was part of their routine. I remember watching her 10-month-old sitting in the stroller as her mother pushed her down a tree-lined street. There was a noticeable wind in the air, and as it blew around her, the baby reached out as if to grab it, harness it, and hold it close. My friend and I walked through the wind as if it were nothing, but this little girl was so excited by the air that was skipping and bouncing in front of her. She was giggling, daring to grasp onto this ethereal joy. She was so young, and perhaps because of her age, not in spite of it, she was thrilled with the simplistic excitement of wind.

Use these first few years to introduce your child to nature, to the outdoors, and to the community around her. You're building a lifelong love of the environment and giving her cognitive and social tools she'll use for years to come.

What Is Nature-Deficit Disorder?

While I was interviewing parents and teachers for this chapter, one teacher's response struck a chord in me. She said, "Nature-deficit disorder is a real problem with our kids today."

Excuse me? Nature-deficit disorder? Is that even a real thing? I dug around a little. Yup, evidently it is. In fact, it's even been written about, extensively. Howard Gardner, the psychologist behind the educational theory of multiple intelligences, added "naturalistic intelligence" to his list of various learning styles when he realized that a child's ability to thrive in nature is a wonderful and sought-after characteristic and is just as necessary as visual, auditory, and interpersonal intelligences.

Journalist and author Richard Louv coined the term *nature-deficit disorder.* Although it is not a medically diagnosed condition, it refers to behavioral problems, especially in children, that arise from spending too much time indoors. He argued that because our children are spending more and more time indoors, they are losing health benefits as well as social skills.

Louv examined the benefits of nature, explaining that "unlike television, nature does not steal time; it amplifies it. . . . Nature inspires creativity in a child by demanding visualization and the full use of the senses." Educator Michael Bentley furthered this argument by pointing out that more and more kids are spending sedentary hours after school watching television or playing video games. With all the technology available, many children gravitate toward a game on their iPad® or a show on television before they electively go outside. By constantly staying inside and choosing sedentary activities, kids are doing more damage than they know. Besides offsetting a higher risk for obesity and other health issues, having exposure to nature actually improves a child's attention and focus, says Bentley.

But so many older children choose to spend their free time indoors and on the computer. This pattern of behavior comes from a learned practice; a toddlerhood that doesn't include nature can easily turn into an indoor childhood.

The Benefits of Taking Your Baby Outside

There are many advantages to spending time outdoors with your child. Richard Louv pointed out that "stress levels, attention-deficit hyperactivity disorder, cognitive functioning—and more—are positively affected by time spent in nature."

In addition, by taking your baby outdoors, you're giving her the opportunity to expand her vocabulary; you'll automatically have dozens of new words to use, thereby giving your child a head start on language. Show her everything, but take it slow. Actually, the very act of taking her out into a natural setting will, all of a sudden, slow the world down. Put your cell phone in your pocket in case of emergencies, but turn off the sound and switch it to vibrating mode. Put your crawling baby down onto a pile of leaves. Take her outside during a light snowfall and let the snow grace her face. Dare her to jump in puddles.

Don't always go outside with an agenda. Sure, my son loves to kick a ball or draw with sidewalk chalk, but sometimes, just going outside and wandering is just as important. Our brains need some downtime. Researchers have explained that being idle "allows the circuitry to develop, to let the brain take what it already knows and think, reflect, and change." Give your child a chance to slow down when you're outside.

A spur-of-the-moment decision to go outdoors with no specific purpose can lead to simple pleasures and discoveries for you and your baby.

When my son was learning to walk, he used to push a toy fire truck around our block. On one corner was a pond with fish, and it was his favorite spot to stop. We had to pause and take a look at the fish every time we went outside. I could've been there for 30 seconds and moved on, and honestly, sometimes I didn't want to sit there for five minutes looking at one fish swim around a tiny artificial pond. But he did. To him, it was just perfect.

If there is some adventure or outdoor activity that you used to enjoy before you became a parent, don't rule it out immediately. For example, consider whether you could take your baby along to your community garden or on a monthly hike you used to take with friends. This way, you're integrating your baby into activities that you already enjoy.

You'll notice that most of the outdoor activities at the end of this chapter are simple and require very few materials. That's the point of being outside. The environment is entertaining enough; don't clutter it with too many toys and other distractions.

The Benefits of Community Outings

It's one thing to take your baby into the woods for a hike alone or with just family and close friends around. However, it can be very overwhelming for new parents to think about taking their babies out into the wider community, be it a quick trip to the store, a meal at a restaurant, or a social event. When my son was about six weeks old, I decided to venture to Target. We drove the half hour to the store, and I got the stroller out and attached the car seat. I had a change of clothes for him, extra diapers, and a blanket. I was ready. We strolled by the women's clothing. Maybe I could browse for a few minutes? Glimpses of my old life started to tease me.

But then he started crying. He was hungry.

I panicked. Where was I supposed to nurse him? I didn't have my nursing pillow; where could we go to sit comfortably and privately? I practically ran out of that store, put him back in the car, and drove home. I was totally freaking out.

When I told this story to more experienced moms, they all had suggestions. "Dressing rooms are great for nursing!" "Just go to the car and nurse, then put him back in the stroller and head back in."

Yes, of course. Why didn't I think of these options? If I'd just found a quiet place to nurse him, he probably would have fallen asleep, and I could have shopped peacefully. But I let the stress get to me and left the store before I could think through a solution.

Sometimes we get so stressed that we just don't think about the obvious and easy solutions. We only think, *What if he screams? What if he gets hungry?* This can be especially overwhelming when we have both a toddler and an infant. *What if my toddler isn't patient while the baby is getting fed or changed? What if my toddler doesn't listen and has a meltdown?* But we have to push past our fears. It's so important for our baby's happiness and for ours. We have to leave our houses.

Benefits for babies

Dr. Harvey Karp advocates for newborns to be taken out of the quiet home environment. Because the womb is loud and jostling, an environment with more stimulation is actually better for a baby than keeping her in a quiet space. White noise such as children playing or restaurant chatter helps infants sleep. Dr. Karp argues, "The womb is louder than a vacuum cleaner, 24/7. And so to put them in a quiet room and tiptoe around . . . it's sensory deprivation. It drives them crazy."

As your baby gets older, social outings will help her to become familiar with diverse surroundings, expose her to different types of people, and provide the chance to build background schema about various community experiences (see Chapter 1). These outings need not have lofty community goals; just the act of going out means you're exposing your child to the larger community.

Community outings will help your children become familiar with diverse surroundings, expose her to different types of people, and provide the chance to build background schema.

Volunteer work or other services that you used to perform pre-baby can be a great way to continue to enjoy these activities and expose your child to the benefits of community service. For example, take your baby in her stroller on a community walk to raise money for AIDS research. Or take her to a fair that raises awareness of global climate change. By raising her to participate in these activities, you're showing that your family values community service. That will be an immeasurable gift to your child.

Benefits for parents

Going out into the community is important to a parent's happiness as well as a baby's welfare. Short outings, like going to stores and restaurants, will help you stay connected to the adult world, but so will friendships and social get-togethers. Finding a group of some sort—for example, new moms or adoptive parents—can do wonders for your well-being. New friendships will make you feel calmer, stronger, and less alone in this new and sometimes stressful circumstance of being a parent. Do what you can to keep your friends in your life. They're helping you stay healthy and happy, and at the same time you're expanding your own community.

There are many ways to do this. As an alternative to a "new parents" group, you might find a regular group of another kind. For example, perhaps you have a set of childless friends you used to like to hang out with who might welcome having a youngster in their midst for a few hours. Your baby will get their attention, and they'll get a fun change of pace!

A Tip from Sarahlynne

Taking Your Baby Out

- **If you're breast-feeding, try to nurse before you leave the house.** If you'll be nursing in public, bring a nursing cover. It covers your entire front and makes nursing in public a discreet and easy activity.
- **If you're bottle-feeding, bring extra formula for the outing.** Powdered formula can fit into portable containers and can be mixed with bottled water. Preprepared formula is also a convenient option.
- **Bring bottled water for yourself.** You're doing a lot of work here!
- **Take along extra outfits.** Bring one or two for the baby and perhaps an extra top for you. Always bring more diapers and wipes than you think you'll need and keep them in the car. Trust me. You'll need them when you least expect it.
- **Limit the toys.** Take a few toys with you, but remember that talking to your baby and taking her out of her car seat carrier are wonderful ways to bond and connect! (See Chapter 2.)
- **Keep her cozy and comfortable.** Chances are she'll sleep for part of the outing. This is awesome but won't always happen.
- **Remember to play.** If your baby has been in the stroller or car seat for the majority of the outing, make a point to play and interact with her when you return home.
- **Bring along a carrier.** If you have a baby who needs or wants to be carried on outings, purchase a wrap or baby carrier so you can easily switch her from car seat to carrier, where she'll be more content.
- **As your child grows, encourage her to walk.** Have her walk instead of using the stroller, whenever she can. It gives her a sense of independence, teaches her boundaries, and helps her to be a part of the community, not just an observer.
- **When she is walking, always hold hands.** Make a game out of crossing the street. For example, you could say, "Freeze! Look left and look right! No cars! Yay! Let's go!" Then run across the street holding hands.

Teaching opportunities

When you do feel comfortable going out in the world, there's so much to do! Take your baby to the grocery store, for a stroll around the neighborhood, to the post office, to the bank, and to the mall. Holiday time at the mall is especially exciting; all the lights and sparkles can be fantastic stimulation for her eyes and ears. Remember to follow your baby's cues; if she seems overstimulated, switch the venue. Don't worry too much at this point about "kid-friendly" activities. There will be plenty of time for that. At this age, taking her anywhere is exciting. I remember the first time my son realized the grocery store was not a place he wanted to frequent. He was about 18 months old. It took that long.

Kids' Books about Community Helpers

- *Career Day* by Anne Rockwall and Lizzy Rockwall
- *A Day in the Life of a Police Officer* by Linda Hayward
- *Delivering Your Mail: A Book about Mail Carriers* by Ann Owen
- *The Fire Cat* by Esther Averill
- *I Stink!* by Kate and Jim McMullan
- *My Teacher's Secret Life* by Stephen Krensky
- *Richard Scarry's Busy, Busy Town* by Richard Scarry
- *When I Grow Up* by P. K. Hallinan

But the good news is, when children get a little older, they want to interact in these places, not just look and observe. Once my son turned two, he started to enjoy the grocery store again; we could do a "treasure hunt" for various objects, and that fascinated him and kept him engaged. Once your toddler can interact with you during these outings, use them for teaching moments. For example, now that I have two children, my son is often walking while I push my daughter in the stroller. So, to keep parking lots safe but also engaging, as I hold his hand I ask him to lead me. "Where is Mommy's car? Do you remember what color it is? Can you find it?" Try to do at least one outing a day. We do ours in the mornings, when everyone is well rested and patient!

During these outings, seeing a favorite community helper can spark some lively talk and open the window for community education. For example, if your child loves to spot a fire truck, you might help him learn about a firefighter's job. See the What Now? sidebar above for a list of children's books about community helpers.

Outdoor Activities for Your Baby

There are activities here for all climates. Take your baby outside whenever you can, whenever the weather is acceptable enough to play outside. Remember sunscreen and a sun hat if it's warm or sunny. In colder or windy weather, pay attention to her movement. If your baby is in the stroller, she's going to be colder than you. An extra blanket and snuggly hat will be a comfy addition and keep her happy while you stroll. An older toddler who is running around still needs mittens (if she won't tear them off!) and a hat, especially in windy or cold weather.

Activities for Ages 0–1

- Nature's touch and smell. Introduce the softness of a flower petal, the sweet smell of a garden, the roughness of the pavement—all incredible sensations to your baby.
- Hiking. Put your baby in a baby carrier and go for a hike. Point out the trees, the water, and the big rocks.
- Swinging. Find the infant swings at the playground. Don't be surprised if your baby falls asleep in the swing!
- Strolling. Go for a walk in the stroller and point out objects your child loves. For my son, it was the garbage truck!
- Grassy or snowy pleasure. Put your crawling infant on the grass to let her feel the softness and plush texture. When it snows, bundle her up and sit her in the snow for a few minutes, letting her feel the icy touch of winter.
- Floating. On a hot summer day, purchase an infant boat and float with her in the pool (using safety precautions, of course!).
- Spray park. Go to a local sprinkler park, and move her around the park. Start at the seated "sprays" and help her play at the water tables.

Activities for Ages 1–3

- Nature treasure hunt. Take a backpack and collect your findings, or just look and touch along the way. Either allow your child to choose what you collect or give her a list with pictures before you leave the house. Treasures could include leaf, rock, flower, tree (some things you can't take home!), potted plant, dog, and park bench. Make some things easy to find and others more difficult. Add to or subtract from the list each time, making it challenging but fun for your child.
- Spraying nature. Fill a spray bottle with water and food coloring. Spray the snow or rain puddles. Make patterns in the snow, or create multicolored "fireworks" in puddles.

- Freezing guesses. In the winter, use containers of different sizes and fill them with water. Let your child add some food coloring to each, and then place them outside when the temperature is below freezing. Have your child guess which will freeze first. This works best when there's a large difference between sizes of the containers. Check throughout the day to see who is winning, and at the end, explain that a larger body of water will take longer to freeze. (Dr. Patricia Wynne, mother of two)
- Bug detectives. Take a magnifying glass outside and inspect insects.
- Bird watching. Bring out the binoculars and identify the birds you see.
- Nature bracelet. Using a piece of tape, preferably two inches or wider, make a bracelet for your child with the sticky side out. Go for a nature walk and invite your child to collect things and stick them to the bracelet. (Dr. Patricia Wynne, mother of two)
- Fun in the park. Go to a public park that is near a body of water, and feed the ducks, if allowed, or follow your child's lead to another activity.
- Buried treasure. Take a few pennies outside and bury them in a special place. Go back a few days later and see if they are still there!
- Rock maze. Place some rocks or leaves in a pattern on the ground and move a little car or truck through it.
- Weather talk. Encourage your child to acknowledge if it's hot or cold, or if it's "raining," "sunny," or "cloudy." Talk about the details of each particular weather pattern. Cut out construction paper in the shape of a sun, cloud, and raindrop. Attach Velcro to the back, and make a weekly weather chart. Each day, have your child choose the appropriate weather picture to put on the chart. After a week, she can look for weather patterns.
- Walking up and down hills. This is great practice for your growing toddler.
- Water hose. Gently spray your toddler, or let her spray the sidewalk, or you!
- Backyard or public sprinklers. Chase the sprinklers around, trying to run from the water, or run right into it!
- Cloud painting. Look at the clouds and encourage your child to describe the shape of each one. Together, create a story about the cloud shapes.
- Variety of outdoor venues. Expose your child to streams, apple orchards, farms, lakes, and forests if possible. All provide distinctive stimulation and can be especially exciting if your child has seen these places in books but never in real life.

(continued)

- Kazoo. Take your child outside with a kazoo. Each time your child hears a bird tweet, she can blow her kazoo. She can also imitate different bird and animal sounds, depending on the wildlife that is around your home! (Neal G., father of two)

Activities for Older Toddlers

- Nature journal. Talk about what you see on your walk, and either stop and sketch some of the objects or go home and do the same. (Rebecca Irwin Slater, MA, elementary education/multiple subject credential)
- Searching for shapes. Take a nature walk and look for just triangles, just squares, just cylinders, or just circles.
- Color journal. Take a piece of paper outside with a green, blue, and red crayon. Every time you see something in nature that corresponds to one of your colors, have your child draw it on the paper. You can write the matching word.
- Acorn collection. Gather some acorns with the heads attached and some without. Using a Sharpie maker, draw faces on the acorns and create acorn people. Then have a parade or have the acorn people go swimming in puddles. (Dr. Patricia Wynne, mother of two)
- Puddle-jumping. Explain the differences between liquids and solids by stating that solids can be held in your hand while liquids fall through. Have your child identify as many liquids and solids as she can while outside. (Dr. Patricia Wynne, mother of two)
- Bird feeder. Roll pinecones in peanut butter (if your child has a peanut allergy, try soy nut butter) and then in birdseed. Thread a pipe cleaner through the cone and create a hanger. Or use a pipe cleaner bent to look like a candy cane and string Cheerios onto it to hang on a branch for the birds. Then, watch for bird visitors and observe their behavior. (Anne D., preschool educator and grandmother)
- Photographs. Take pictures of items your child chooses, and then name and discuss them when you return. For example, your child may take pictures of an interesting cloud shape, a beautiful flower, or an old, rundown fence. (Rebecca Irwin Slater, MA, elementary education/multiple subject credential)
- Gardening. Help your child to plant her own flower or herb, and teach her about the daily care of plants. If it's too cold outside, use a small pot on the windowsill. When the weather is warmer, transplant the seedling into the ground and continue the fun outdoors.
- Leaf wreath. Cut out a piece of construction paper into a ring shape. Have your child collect leaves outside, and then come in and glue them onto the paper. This project is especially beautiful in the fall.

- Weight experiments. Find a few objects outside with varying weights—for example, a leaf, a rock, an acorn, and a piece of grass. Line them all up on the driveway you've blockaded from traffic. One by one, have your child throw them. Which one goes the farthest? Which one barely moves? Why?
- Skipping stones. Toss rocks across a lake and watch the water flicker as they skip. Don't worry if you can't do this well. Just point out the ripple effect to your child as the pebble sinks.
- Shadow tracing. On a sunny day, take some chalk or markers and paper and trace shadows outside. Trace a small tree, and then wait five minutes. Trace the shadow again and see how far it's moved. Explain what a shadow is and why it moves. (Dr. Patricia Wynne, mother of two)
- Starry night. On black construction paper, use chalk to draw dots of constellations such as the Big Dipper and Orion. Show your child the picture and then ask her to connect the dots into the shape of the constellation. Later, on a clear night, go outside and see if you can match the real constellation to the drawing.
- Pressing flowers. Pick some wildflowers and dry them between two pieces of wax paper, closed in a book. Then, try to find their names online or in a book.

Community Activities for Your Baby

Try to take your baby out into the community as often as her comfort will allow it. Remember that community activities encompass many kinds of outings and can be simple!

Activities for Ages 0–1

- Boys' or girls' morning out. When my son was only a few months old, my husband made a point of taking him and our dog on a community adventure every Saturday morning. It became their ritual. Often, they just went to the dump to throw away garbage or to the bank. But it was "their thing," and I know my husband loved the time alone with the baby.
- People-watching. Go to a park and let your infant watch the big kids play.

(continued)

- Errands and daily life. Go to the library, have a quiet chat with the librarian, and choose a few books to take home. Go to the bank and make a withdrawal. Take your baby with you when you get the mail, and let her hold a few letters. When the fire trucks, mail trucks, or garbage trucks go by, talk about the sounds, sights, and smells of these community vehicles!
- Pet store. Go to a pet store and discover the fish in the tanks or the cats and dogs awaiting adoption.
- Playground adventure. When your baby is learning to walk, take her to a playground and stand her up next to a structure. My son used to love picking up the mulch on the ground at the playground and piling it onto the bottom of the slide.
- Bookstore. Some bookstores have awesome children's sections with train tables, plush pillows, and a few toys. They may even have a free story hour for little ones and their parents. This outing can be a great one for meeting new friends, for both baby and mom or dad!

Activities for Ages 1–3

- Grocery store helper. Open a plastic bag and have your child put the fruits and vegetables inside. Or, as you travel through the store, invite her to try to find her favorite crackers or cereal. At the register, explain the process of paying for the food, bagging it, and taking it to the car.
- Store treasure hunt. Go to a store, and depending on your child's age, "hunt" for a few things. With a young child, focus on one object, like a balloon or a ball. An older child can have a picture list of three or four items, like a doll, a box of diapers, a tube of toothpaste, and some toilet paper. Bonus: Manage the treasure hunt around things you already need, and you'll have an instant helper!
- Garbage truck. Take a walk in the neighborhood when you know the garbage truck is making its rounds. Have your child try to find it, or guess which corner it will turn next! Count the number of times it makes an appearance as well.
- Pattern search. In the car, ask your child to count all the green cars she sees. In the store, she can look for all the girls, boys, or babies. (Teach her how to discreetly point these out to you.) A younger child can tell you whenever she sees the chosen "item," but an older child can count and see how high she can get before you return home. Expand your child's vocabulary with objects and adjectives such as garbage truck, blonde hair, dark hair, motorcycle, and so forth.
- Fire station. Many communities host open houses at the fire stations. These are usually held in the fall or spring. Young children are often allowed to talk to firefighters, touch the fire trucks, and see the inside of a station.

- Pumpkin patch or apple orchard. Even young toddlers can enjoy a hay ride, picking apples off a tree, or carrying a small pumpkin.
- Community pool, spray park, or natural site. If you find a public beach at a lake, ocean, or river, you can give your child both the outdoors and the community exposure! Let her play in the sand and water, going at her own pace, at her comfort level. Show her the lifeguards, and explain their job and the basics of water safety.
- Practice community holidays like Halloween or Independence Day. Pretend "trick-or-treat" around the house to show your child the process. If you're planning to attend a fireworks display, draw fireworks, practice making the sounds, or even splatter paint in bright colors on black paper to explain what fireworks look like.
- Finding the holiday houses. Communities are decorated for each holiday, such as Valentine's Day, Halloween, Thanksgiving, and Christmas, so use this as a teaching opportunity. Read books and talk about the upcoming holiday, and then have your child point out the decorations on people's houses or in stores. Some toddler gyms even have special holiday parties that you can attend for a small fee.
- Community hunt. Invite a few friends (and their parents) along. Find a small strip mall where there are a few storefronts. Tell the kids you will be looking for specific items, for instance, a pumpkin and scarecrow in the fall, or a snowflake or snowman decoration in the winter. Practice holding hands and walking slowly from storefront to storefront, looking for your treasure items.
- Museums. Even young toddlers can enjoy the open space of a gallery. Many museums offer story hours during the weekday mornings, educational "classes" or shows meant for toddlers, or even rooms for toddler play and discovery.
- Farming. Take your child's stuffed animals outside. Use sticks to build a fence for horse pastures or pig pens. Use sand pails to milk cows. (Dr. Patricia Wynne, mother of two)
- Library trip. Invite your child to look at books with you, choose the ones she wants to bring home, and check them out herself! Even two-year-olds can become very comfortable with the routine of this activity.

(continued)

- Community member role-playing. Point out fire trucks, police cars, garbage trucks, and mail trucks. Discuss the colors of the trucks, their sizes, and their sounds. Ask your child to pretend to be a fire truck, a garbage truck, or a police car. What different sounds should she make? When you visit a store, make a point to have a short chat with the clerk at the register. Modeling friendly behavior shows your child the importance of each person and their role in the community. An additional benefit is that if your child ever gets separated from you in a store, she will know who she can ask for help.
- Choosing and purchasing items. This game is great to play at home for practice, and then act out in the real world. At home, take turns playing the store owner. In the community, invite your toddler to help put groceries on the conveyer belt, and even guess how much the items will cost.
- Community collage. Once your child is aware of community people and vehicles, cut out community pictures from magazines and glue them onto construction paper.
- Community drama. Get a bunch of hats, such as a baseball cap, a construction helmet, and a police hat. Imagine scenarios for your child to play out. For example, place some blocks on the floor and say, "The mayor wants to build a skyscraper! Which community helper can do this job?" Your child can pick the construction helmet and help build the tower.
- Stopping traffic. Have one person pretend to be the police officer, and the other the motorist (on a Big Wheel or tricycle). Make a cardboard STOP sign, or allow your child to yell, "Red light! Green light!" to signal the motorist to stop and go. (Dr. Patricia Wynne, mother of two)
- Peeking into places that don't **seem** child-friendly. My son loves to look in the door of the auto shop we pass on the way to the post office.

Notes:

Chapter Preview

- The risks of exposing your baby to TV and other screen time
- So-called educational TV programs
- How to deal with the screen time in your baby's life
- Healthier entertainment options

Chapter 9

The Consequences of Screen Time

Will you be turning on the television for your child who is under two? Read this chapter first! According to Kidshealth.org, two-thirds of infants and toddlers watch a screen an average of two hours a day. But the high proportion of young watchers doesn't make that fact acceptable. The American Academy of Pediatrics advises that there should be *no* screen time until the age of two, and after that, no more than two hours per day. The research supporting this claim is startling.

We should be much more wary of our kids' screen time. And if possible, we should find other entertainment outlets for our kids when they are very young.

How Television Affects Your Baby

We already know that during the first few years of life a baby's brain is developing rapidly. However, television watching is not the activity to teach your young baby. A baby cannot see beyond 12 inches in his first months, and he cannot track the objects that move across the screen. Television shows move quickly, and infants cannot tell the difference between a commercial and a storyline on a show. Your baby doesn't know where the story starts or ends. To him, each change of the screen is a new story. So he's not following a story or learning a life lesson. His eyes are just darting around the screen as he scans bright lights and quickly changing images. That's why a baby looks "glued" to the television set while he watches, an activity unsuitable for his developing attention span. In fact, when a baby looks like he's "loving" a show, in reality, he's just being forced to look at it. He can't physically tear his eyes away.

We want our young children to choose what they look at; we don't want to force them into staring at something that is overstimulating and ultimately distracting. So we give them one toy or one book, chat with them, or make silly faces at them. As we've seen in previous chapters, these activities have excellent benefits for cognitive and social development. However, when we turn on the television for children under two years old, they are not learning at all. They are, in fact, unable to concentrate on the screen and may feel overwhelmed. The screen also may have negative effects on their development.

Will TV increase the risk of ADHD?

During the last few years, there has been lots of debate over a possible connection between screen time for babies and an ADHD diagnosis in later childhood. Here's a startling finding from a study led by pediatrician Dimitri Christakis: "Early exposure to television was associated with subsequent attentional problems . . . even while controlling for a number of potential confounding factors such as socioeconomic status and gestational age." Christakis's study set off a firestorm of controversial discussion. Consequently, other researchers tried to replicate these results without success. However, the results got parents to pay more attention to how often their young children were in front of the screen.

ADD (attention deficit disorder) and ADHD (attention-deficit hyperactivity disorder) are behavioral disorders that manifest themselves with symptoms such as the inability to pay attention to details, carelessness, difficulty with sustained attention, listening problems, excessive running or talking, and problems with interrupting or distractibility. ADD/ADHD is not easy to deal with and often requires individual education plans, special educational instruction, and specific behavioral plans. It can take years to find a strategy that helps a child with ADD/ADHD to be successful in school and social situations. Although there are many other factors that can cause ADD/ADHD, such as genetics, smoking during pregnancy, and other health issues such as premature birth, according to Kidshealth.org research has shown that a lot of early television watching may also be a correlating factor.

Keep in mind that research is still ongoing, and causes of ADD/ADHD are not entirely known. However, the Centers for Disease Control and Prevention revealed that the number of "children with a parent-reported ADHD diagnosis increased by 22% between 2003 and 2007." Now that some studies have hinted at a relationship between early television viewing and attention problems, and ADHD diagnosis has recently been reported to be on the rise, why not err on the side of caution and turn off the screens when our children are babies?

The constant television household

But what if the television is on as background noise? Is that such a big deal? Actually, yes. Ellen Wartella, a scholar who has studied the effect of media on child development, calls this a *constant television household*. Research suggests that some potential negative consequences for growing up in such a household might include lower literacy scores and a later onset of reading.

Although screens may seem unavoidable in the home, there are ways to deemphasize them in a child's daily routine.

Of course, although you want to foster your child's imaginative play, there may inevitably be some times when the TV will be on. In that case, try to limit your child's exposure by putting him in a portable crib away from the television or allowing him to play in a different room so he's not distracted by the colorful images flashing across the screen. Keep the volume low so that the background noise is kept to a minimum.

What Is Your Little One Watching?

TV ads: Yup, they're targeting your toddler

Do you remember TV commercials from when you were a kid? I do. Whenever I saw a Barbie doll driving around in her beautiful pink Porsche or playing in her Dream House, I was immediately jealous. The girls in the commercial were so cutely dressed, having so much fun together, and playing with the most beautiful, perky toys. I was no longer satisfied with my shoebox filled with a few pieces of Barbie furniture and handmade accessories. (I used to cut up old sweatpants to make "sleeping bags" for my Barbies.) I wanted what was on TV. I thought that what I had wasn't good enough; I needed more.

Marketers spend $16 billion per year on advertising products to children, and by the age of two, a toddler can recognize a brand and even show his parents that he wants it. So before your child can really talk, he's being marketed to. Marketers want him to be able to know what he likes by name. It's not enough to like trains, he has to like (and want) Thomas the Tank Engine. The more exposed your child is to the media, the more he wants what he sees. Researchers have found that "97% of American children six or under have [toy] products based on TV shows or movies."

But this statistic is important for a different reason. Marketers want kids to be enthralled with the commercials. Earlier this chapter mentioned that infants can't tell the difference between a TV show and a commercial. But toddlers can. Clinical psychologist Mary Pipher comments that television and media marketing can teach children to be unhappy with what they already have; TV commercials teach them that "they should indulge every whim, meet every need and buy every product," that products can solve complex human problems, and that buying is important. When I was a kid, I became instantly dissatisfied when I saw a commercial for the latest Barbie accessory. I was no longer happy with what my imagination could create. It's the same with our little ones. Our toddlers watch TV, see toys they want, decide what brand will satisfy them, and lose all form of creativity when it comes to choosing a toy. Advertisers have decided for them. This type of reaction may be inevitable, but do you really want to have this conversation with your toddler if you can avoid it?

The good news is that you can prevent your child from seeing too many advertisements. If you turn on the television in your home, try to rent movies and television shows from the library or pick shows "on demand." They have far fewer commercials.

So-called educational programming for babies

What about all the shows advertised as "educational" and all the "educational" computer products marketed to infants and toddlers? Uh oh. Did you notice the word "marketed"? We're back to that again. Let's talk about the effects these shows and products have on our kids. You might be surprised.

Children's television programs: A program that seems to teach numbers and letters with a cute, accompanying storyline can actually be *detrimental* to developing minds. Think one word: conflict. Developmental psychologist Jamie Ostrov and his colleagues followed preschoolers who watched "educational media" over a period of two years. The kids were between two and a half and five years old when the study began. The findings were disturbing. The researchers concluded that "television exposure is associated with the transmission of both physical and relational aggression in gender-specific ways during early childhood. (The boys were more physically aggressive whereas the girls were more relationally aggressive.) This means the kids were more bossy, aggressive, and able to manipulate situations better than their peers who did not watch these shows. But why? Most educational television shows do not include violence of any kind—or so they'd have you believe. But almost always, there is a conflict. Friends argue over a toy, characters voice verbal putdowns, or there is an emotional issue in the character's life. Most of the action is in building this conflict, as in most stories, and in the end, the conflict is resolved.

Books about Kids' TV Time

- *The Elephant in the Living Room: Make Television Work for Your Kids* by Dimitri A. Christakis and Frederick J. Zimmerman
- *Into the Minds of Babes: How Screen Time Affects Children from Birth to Age Five* by Lisa Guernsey
- *Living outside the Box: TV-free Families Share Their Secrets* by Barbara Brock
- *The Other Parent: The Inside Story of the Media's Effect on Our Children* by James P. Steyer

Unfortunately, a young child cannot connect themes in long stories, asserts Ostrov. Therefore, the child remembers only the specific behaviors he saw in the show, not the overall theme that is taught. This means that if a child hears one character call another a name, he may use that same name in a later context.

This study was replicated *four* times with the *same results* each time. So the lesson is to pay attention to the shows your children watch. Take a look at character interactions and how many minutes of the show are devoted to building a conflict, especially if it's character to character. Assume that your child understands more than you think and will repeat the behaviors he sees. And most of all, pay attention to how the conflict is resolved. Do the characters put each other down, ostracize a friend, or use name-calling? If you feel uncomfortable with how a conflict is resolved, change the channel.

Language development videos and DVDs: But what about baby language videos and DVDs? Those are popular and have been around for some time, so they must be beneficial, right? Nope. Not at all. They are merely marketed that way and have been proven to actually be detrimental to your child's language development. A study at the University of Washington reported, "For every hour per day the children spent watching certain baby DVDs and videos, the infants understood an average of six to eight fewer words than infants who did not watch them." As a result of this particular study, Disney, the producer of the Baby Einstein DVDs mentioned in the study, announced a product recall offering refunds to some buyers and ultimately removed the word "educational" from the packaging.

Another study, also performed at the University of Washington, looked at the association of media exposure and language development in infants and toddlers. The researchers interviewed parents about the amount of time the babies watched DVDs marketed to babies, but also documented the time spent on other activities, such as reading, music, and storytelling. Next, the researchers gave the babies the Communicative Development Inventory (CDI), a standard assessment for measuring language development in young children. After synthesizing the data, the researchers found "a large negative association between viewing of baby DVDs/videos and vocabulary acquisition in children age 8 to 16 months." Specifically, babies who watched one hour per day of these DVDs as opposed to none at all had a 17-point decrease in their score on the CDI. The researchers argued that many factors need to be considered here, because parental interviews—a huge part of data collection—can be subjective. A clear cause-and-effect conclusion cannot be drawn because other unobserved family factors may be involved in the results.

Even though both these studies had limitations, their strengths are important to note. Many parents show their infants baby DVDs in the hope that they'll develop stronger vocabulary, but the opposite can be true. So when it comes to "language development" DVDs, don't waste your money or your time. They don't help, and they may even do harm. As we've talked about in Chapter 4, language development comes from interaction and parental response, which can be easily accomplished without a DVD.

Managing Your Baby's Screen Time

High stakes, right? And yet, most of us will admit that our toddlers, and maybe even our infants, watch TV. Screens are everywhere. They're on our smart phones, in our cars, and on computers. Who hasn't turned on *Sesame Street* so they could cook dinner or take a shower? And who hasn't allowed their younger child to watch his older sister's show just because it was too hard to amuse the toddler while the preschooler enjoyed her screen time? One alternative is to allow the older child to watch television while the younger one naps, but that's not always possible. And sometimes, television can give an exhausted parent a bit of rest. I've definitely been there. I do turn on the television for my son on a regular basis. It is monitored, and we are consistent about the screen time allowed in his day, but it is part of his life.

According to the Kidshealth.org statistics, most parents aren't heeding the guidelines of the American Academy of Pediatrics. Of course, some children don't watch any screens for the first two years and some beyond even that, but for most of us, that isn't an option we're willing to consider. Occasional TV watching is not going to harm a young brain. Sometimes television relaxes the parent too, and a happy parent is extremely beneficial for a child. So, if you know television or screen time is going to have a place in your house, the next question becomes this: *What can I do to make the effects less detrimental to my child's development?*

In your baby's first year, television really isn't necessary. He's not learning anything from it, he can't pay attention to it, and it may be hurting his ability to develop a strong attention span and ability to focus. Furthermore, any screen time takes away from time that the child could be interacting with other babies or his caregiver. So try to go as long as you can without turning on the TV in front of your infant.

Between the ages of one and two, monitor, monitor, monitor. Again, your baby really doesn't need TV, but if you decide to turn it on, choose slow-paced shows and try to watch with him. Be aware of how your child reacts to television and act accordingly. If he watches a couple of shows and then afterward becomes erratic, more volatile, or more prone to tantrums, it may be time to dial down the time.

Once your child turns two, television may be used in moderation, up to two hours a day, but not all at once! Try scheduling TV watching in half-hour increments. When the child is this age, the worry becomes less about brain development and more about sitting him in front of a screen when he could be playing outside or getting exercise or mental stimulation in a more productive way. As noted by Drs. Brazelton and Greenspan, when kids watch too much they "miss out on the give-and-take that mobilizes the central nervous system into integrated pathways and leads to growth." They also miss out on critical social interactions with peers and caregivers.

Most of us do the best we can to tailor our child's screen time to our family's lifestyle and values. You might, like I did, choose to use television as part of your child's schedule. The sidebar offers some tips to keep in mind.

A Tip from Sarahlynne

Ten Television Tips

1. **Be aware of where the television is in the house.** Put the TV in the living room, where it can be monitored. A small child does not need one in his room. If he watches TV in his room, he learns that this is an "alone" activity, not a social one. That may not be the message you wish to send.
2. **Try not to use television or movies in the car.** Being in the car is an entertaining activity; it doesn't need to be accompanied by television. Invite your child to look out the window and notice the world pass by. Play "I Spy," give him a book or toys, or encourage him to find things. My son loves finding trucks and trains while we drive, especially when we pull up right next to one. We always have music in the car, and sometimes my son will sing along with the radio. Keep a stash of books, snacks, and toys in the car as well, in case you get stuck in traffic or your child wants to get out of the car before you've reached your destination. Playing a story on CD as another alternative.
3. **Use restaurants for social time, not screen time.** Yes, it's more stressful if your child doesn't have an electronic babysitter at a restaurant. Yes, at first, you'll have to leave earlier and eat faster. But you will be able to engage your child in conversation and teach him appropriate restaurant behavior. This is a life skill that he can start to learn early. If you want to, bring small books or a little toy, or let him use the crayons the restaurant provides with the children's menu. He can use these to entertain himself and watch what's going on around him. If he never uses a screen at a restaurant and has no idea it's even an option, he may surprise you by rising to your expectations with appropriate behavior.
4. **Even though TV isn't recommended before age two, give yourself a break occasionally.** We all need relief sometimes. Ever been sick and taking care of a toddler? Just monitor your child's viewing and keep it short. By giving yourself a break when you need it, limiting the amount of time your child spends in front of the TV, and monitoring what your child is watching, you can be confident you're doing the best you can when it comes to screen time.
5. **Schedule TV watching and stick to the predetermined time.** A friend of mine allows her daughter to watch in the early afternoon before nap. My son watches his shows in the late afternoon, after playtime and before dinner. The rest of the day, he usually doesn't approach the screen; he knows it's not time. He sometimes asks for TV during other parts of the day but isn't surprised if I say no.

6. **Be very aware of the shows your child is watching.** Make sure the programs have a slow pace, only minor confrontations, and satisfactory resolutions. Keep an eye out for any violence, physical or emotional. Watch with your child when you can, making TV watching interactive. And introduce only a few shows to your child. If you keep his TV world small, it can't compete with the wonders of the real world.
7. **Remember that your child sees more than you think.** So, if you're watching the news and your toddler is playing with his blocks, don't think that he's not glancing at the screen full of fires, violence, and scary headlines. Reserve the scary stuff—or, if possible, all your own TV time—for after he goes to bed. Also, be aware of your own screen time usage. Make a family rule that there are no screens at the dinner table. If you're playing or talking with your child and your phone beeps at you, make a point of telling your child, "We're busy; we'll find out who called later."
8. **Use television to your child's advantage.** When you discuss a favorite concept with your child, you can make television a springboard for discussion and activities. For example, if your child loves train shows, read about trains every day and talk about trains every time you see one.
9. **Turn screen time into bonding moments.** Television does provide an opportunity to snuggle with your little one, chat about the show, and spend some time together. He may enjoy acting out the storyline with his toys (just as he does with books!) and might connect to the characters and their emotions. There are many other bonding opportunities for parent and baby (see Chapter 2), but if you're choosing the right shows, your child watches it only occasionally, and you can manage to sometimes watch together, then you're on the right track.
10. **Be prepared to break the rules.** My son has had a couple of miserable sick days, and on those days, he watched a few extra episodes of *Sesame Street*. It's a rarity, but it has happened. Give yourself a break if your child is sick. Do what you need to do to help him feel better. A sick toddler is no fun, and if other family members are sick too, you've got a challenging situation on your hands. Take it day by day and do your best while everyone is recovering. Sometimes, situations are tough, but they pass, and your baby's schedule will resume as soon as he feels better.

Healthier Entertainment Options

I have to admit, I watched a lot of TV when my son was a newborn. He was nursing often, and since I needed both hands to nurse, television provided welcome entertainment. It worked well for a few months. He was so small that he just focused on what was in front of him, so he didn't even know the TV was on. But when he started to perk up at the sound of the *Sex and the City* theme song, I got nervous. I realized he was attending to the screen. It was time to turn it off. I soon realized I needed another outlet for entertainment, one that provided stimulation for both him and me and offered a change from playing on the living room floor.

Easy alternatives at home

Although screens are everywhere, the home offers so much screen-free entertainment for an infant and toddler. (As a reminder, just take a look at the activities in the other chapters!) It's a transition, but just like all of the other transitions you've made as a parent, it's doable.

Instead of using TV as a babysitter, this mother has kept her baby busy with a toy. One strategy in keeping a baby occupied is to hand the baby a new toy when the old one is no longer interesting.

Keep some activities ready for when you're frustrated, tired, or just needing a few minutes of peace. Infants enjoy bouncy seats, play mats, jumpers, and swings, but if that's getting old, try handing your baby some clothing accessories or a box filled with fun household items that he can discover. New textures are fascinating as well. Crawling infants love to climb; put some pillows on the floor or create a little fort that he can dive into. Older infants and toddlers love to copy their parents. Open a cupboard filled with plastic containers and cookie cutters, and watch him pretend to cook. Or allow him to play in your closet. My son loves to take all my shoes out of their boxes, put on my necklaces, and even walk around the room in my high heels. It cracks me up and gives me time to fold laundry.

Stepping out

When my son was about six months old, we started going on play dates with a neighbor a couple of afternoons a week. He was entertained by watching her three young girls play, and I had a chance to chat with a friend. As noted in Chapter 6, we cannot underestimate the power of play dates, even for very small children.

If you work at home, or just need to get some things accomplished on your own, see if you can find an alternative to screen time. You could occasionally tap the power of the play date by swapping time with a close friend. Offer to watch her children for a few hours while she gets some work done, and let her repay the favor. Since you all have already become comfortable with each other at the play dates, it can be a relatively easy transition. Or set your child up with a fun and new activity (like racing cars through an obstacle course set up with cereal boxes for houses and oatmeal grains for a bumpy terrain), and you may be able to steal away for 15 or 20 minutes.

When you're feeling tired of being in the house, don't underestimate the power of going outside! Go for a walk with your baby. He'll love feeling the wind, looking at the sights outside, and hearing the sounds unique to the outdoor environment. When stuck indoors on a cold or rainy day, turn on music for your little one. He'll enjoy the rhythm and beat and will love the sounds of the instruments and melodies. You don't even need to play "baby music." Expose your baby to everything! Classical, swing. Top 40—anything that has a fun beat and melody will be exciting to your child's ears. He may even play better by himself when he has music on in the background.

Basically, it's about scheduling your day with activities that don't include screen time and saving television for a last resort. This can sometimes be hard. I missed television most on the rainy Saturday afternoons that my husband and I used to spend as "movie days." Once our son was born, we started going to indoor play gyms, Barnes & Noble to play with the train sets, or museums. Once, in desperation, we even took him to Toys "R" Us. He had so much fun climbing in and out of the tot-sized trucks and cars.

Going out into the community is a great alternative to screen time. Between iPads®, smart phones, and computers, there is always a "reason" to turn on a screen. But there will be plenty of time in your child's life for him to become fluent in technological devices. Instead, the early years should be focused on hands-on, multisensory experiences as often as possible.

Chapter Preview

- How to keep your baby occupied when you're feeling sick
- The power of a best friend in fostering sibling ties
- Preparing your toddler for a sibling
- Adjusting to the new arrival

Chapter 10

Preparing Your Family for Another Child

It started almost immediately upon returning from the hospital. My son wanted me to play with him, snuggle with him before bedtime, and generally give him the attention he'd grown accustomed to. But now I had a newborn. And she needed lots of attention too. So I had to learn to split my attention, give them both what they needed, but also teach my son that he may have to wait a few minutes at times. And it was hard. It was messy. My son really struggled for the first few months. He acted out, regressed in certain behaviors, and although he was proud of his sister, seemed heartbroken that he couldn't always have my full attention. And I felt so guilty. There was only one of me and two of them, and even though my husband was an awesome help, sometimes I felt like I was always letting one of them down. It took a long time to find a new balance.

If you're preparing to bring a new child into your home, your mind is undoubtedly teeming with all sorts of thoughts. You know what it's like to take care of a child, but how on earth are you going to continue to give that child all that she needs when you have a new baby, who is going to need even more attention? In this chapter, we'll talk about a variety of issues that arise during the time you're expecting your second child as well as the period right after the child arrives.

Caregivers Don't Get Sick Days: How Do You Cope?

Have you ever been sick while taking care of a baby or more than one child? It's super fun. When I was about three months pregnant with my daughter, I was absolutely exhausted. I had about an hour of energy in the morning and then had to sit down and relax before continuing with another activity later in the day. My two-year-old, of course, had leaps and bounds of energy and wanted to run and play all day, as we'd done prior to the pregnancy. I tried playing on the floor with him, but he wanted to kick his soccer ball. I kept thinking, "In a few months I'll have two to take care of! And I'll be up all night!"

Calling on some friends for advice, I learned some great tricks. We scheduled play dates, where I knew my son would have a blast and I could sit on the couch and monitor any conflicts. We went outside to a safe and small playground (being outside always made me feel better), and I could sit on the grass while he ran around with his friends. And when I was very tired, I took a nap while he did and went to bed early. I also began relying on my husband during the exhausting points in my pregnancy. He took on a more active role when he got home from work, taking the lead at bath time and bedtime and giving me a chance to sit in the rocking chair in my son's room. I was still part of the routine, but not having to do everything gave me the chance to still enjoy my son and get a few minutes of rest.

Whatever the reason—pregnancy, general fatigue, or the common cold—when you're not at your best, you'll have an easier time if you've lined up a few backup aids in caring for your youngster. Some of my friends have family members nearby who can take their children if needed. But others live far from family or have partners who can't take time off, and on those days, the hours can seem endless.

A Tip from Sarahlynne

Activities to Occupy Your Child While You're Sick

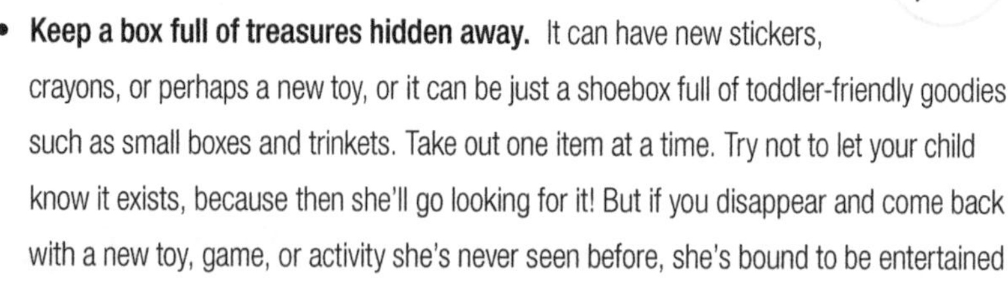

- **Keep a box full of treasures hidden away.** It can have new stickers, crayons, or perhaps a new toy, or it can be just a shoebox full of toddler-friendly goodies such as small boxes and trinkets. Take out one item at a time. Try not to let your child know it exists, because then she'll go looking for it! But if you disappear and come back with a new toy, game, or activity she's never seen before, she's bound to be entertained for some time.

- **Have a dance party.** Is there a song your child could listen to for hours? Turn it on and nurse a cup of tea while your child bounces around. For added fun, give her a hairbrush to use as a microphone, and pretend she's on stage, singing and dancing to an audience.
- **Have a salon day.** Let your toddler braid, brush, and run her hands through your hair. If she'll let you, do the same for her. Teach her how to French-braid, and practice on dolls. Paint her nails and toes. (If your child is a thumb sucker, leave the thumbs unpainted!)
- **Have a dress day from mom's closet.** Take out your high heels, scarves, costume jewelry, and hats. Let her practice walking in heels, wear as much jewelry as she wants, and try on all the hats. Take pictures while she strikes fabulous poses!
- **Make an alphabet scrapbook.** This activity works well with a child who has a beginning grasp of the alphabet. Staple 13 sheets of construction paper together, making 26 pages. Label each page a letter of the alphabet. Go through magazines and newspapers and cut out pictures that begin with each letter. Tape or glue the pictures onto each appropriate page. Bonus: Now your child has her own alphabet dictionary!
- **Make macaroni jewelry.** String ziti or fun-shaped pasta onto string. Color them first with markers to make a pattern.
- **Start an art project.** Arts and crafts are great activities when you're feeling sick. Finger painting, sand art, playing with glue and glitter, and even just coloring are sedentary and quiet but will also mentally stimulate your child.
- **Direct a treasure hunt.** Hide some plastic eggs or plastic containers throughout the backyard or in a room of the house. Sit down and invite your child to find them all as fast as she can. Set a timer to track her progress. Have your child close her eyes and you can hide them again. See if she can beat her record!
- **Be outdoors.** If you're feeling good enough to venture farther, go to a nearby park or playground. Once you're there, your child will be able to run and expend her energy and focus on something other than you. An outing, even if it's only an hour, will make your day go a bit faster.

So what can you do during those rough times when all you really want to do is turn on the television? (And if you do sometimes resort to TV, it's okay.) The key is to find imaginative activities that take little effort on your part but will keep your child entertained and happy. See the sidebar for some gems.

Preparing Your Child for a New Arrival

Okay, so you're mastering the physical challenges of getting ready for a new child. But what about the mental and emotional preparation?

The power of a best friend

Does your toddler have a "best friend," a child she sees a few times a week, with whom she fights, plays, and imagines? (Her definition of a "best friend" may be different from yours!) If so, you're in luck! A best friend can help prepare your child for a sibling.

Fostering sibling relationships: Laurie Kramer and John Gottman, experts in family studies, examined the correlation between toddler friendships and sibling relationships. They noted that toddler "best friendships" require "certain social and emotional competencies" (such as de-escalating conflict, handling frustration, and sharing) that will prepare the child for siblinghood. They found that this is especially true if the children are old enough to engage in cooperative, imaginative play, which requires give-and-take, discussion, and compromise. If a young child has been in a caring relationship with someone other than her parent (such as a best friend), she learns the skills and emotional tools that she can use with her sibling later.

But why does this work with a best friend and not just a bunch of playmates? Because playing with a best friend creates a more intimate relationship than playing with a large group of kids. In a one-on-one friendship, one child will begin to care about the feelings of the other. Your child will come to know her friend's personality and quirks and will have to work at this friendship. She will test her limits, push her buttons, annoy her, and have a fantastic time playing with her. It will be very similar to a sibling relationship. Daycare and playgroup situations alone don't provide this same type of socialization.

The caregiver's influence: Even though Kramer's study is important for revealing the potential of your child's best friend, don't underestimate the power of adult behaviors. First, remember that when a toddler's caregivers show empathy toward others, the child will pick up on this behavior and mimic it with playmates and siblings. Secondly, unlike a parent, who gives love unconditionally, your child will have to work at keeping her friend happy. My son's best friend lives next door. She's three months younger, and they see each other almost every day. Some days they have a great time, but other days they quarrel. And even at age two, they have private jokes. It is amazing to watch. They hug and kiss each other, play together, and of course, argue incessantly over toys and turns.

Encourage your child to develop a strong friendship early on.

The key here is to encourage your child to develop a strong friendship early on. You can do this before the thought of a second child even crosses your mind. You cannot force a friendship on your toddler. However, you can introduce her to a few other children. If she's in daycare or a playgroup, you can observe whom she plays with most of the time and arrange a play date with that child's parents. Your child may or may not choose to strongly befriend the other child after many play dates. Sometimes these relationships happen organically, but other times they just don't.

Telling your child about the new baby

Even if your child has a best friend and is socially prepared, there will still be a large adjustment when the baby arrives. Your child will need a gentle and slow transition, and even if you're careful and attentive, she'll probably have some feelings of jealousy, anger, and frustration. It's important to anticipate these feelings while you're expecting so that you can give your first child the time and attention she needs before you're exhausted and distracted with another one. A pregnancy or the period of waiting for an adoption often provides parents with a wonderful few months of preparatory time that can set the stage for the child's view on the new baby. You can alleviate your child's worries and fears, answer her frequent questions, and complete many changes during this period.

You know your little one better than any expert, and your family circumstances will help you to know when to begin this transition. Keep in mind your child's age. Dr. Penelope Leach encourages parents to share the news about a new baby in the second half of the pregnancy. If you have a child who's not yet two, remember that she probably won't have much of a concept of what you're talking about but will benefit

What NOW?

Some Books about New Arrivals

- *I'm a Big Brother* or *I'm a Big Sister* by Joanna Cole
- *My New Baby and Me: A First Year Record Book for Big Brothers and Sisters* by Metropolitan Museum of Art and Marie Madel Franc-Nohain
- *The New Baby* or *Just My Little Brother and Me* by Mercer Mayer
- *The New Baby Train* by Woody Guthrie
- *The Berenstain Bears' New Baby* by Stan and Jan Berenstain
- *Peter's Chair* by Ezra Jack Keats
- *A Pocketful of Kisses* by Audrey Penn
- *Seeds of Love: For Brothers and Sisters of International Adoption* by Mary Ebejer Petertyl

from all the discussion and excitement. If your child is between two and four, her concept of time is usually still too basic to understand time in terms of months. If there are still several months to wait, she may have no idea what you're talking about.

As an alternative, a few months before the baby's arrival, begin discussing what a new baby means to the family. Tell her that she'll become a big sister, read her "big sister" books, and explain that soon there will be a new baby living in the house. Show her babies when you go out into the community so that she can slowly figure out the concept of "baby." Whenever possible, take her to your prenatal appointments or pre-adoptive counseling sessions and explain to her what's happening. When visiting my doctor during my second pregnancy, I always told my son, "It's time to be a big brother and go hear the baby's heartbeat!" He helped me put my expected daughter's clothes into her dresser drawers and set up her half of the room. If your child is old enough, you can ask her to talk to the baby, or she can even feel the baby kick later in your pregnancy. If you are adopting a child, use the options that are available to you. For example, if you receive pictures or videos of the new baby, show them to your child at opportune times. Or record your family's voices in a "talking" teddy bear and send the toy to your waiting child.

Be excited, but be honest with your toddler, says the American Academy of Pediatrics. Explain that babies cry often, will have to drink a lot of special milk, and will need lots of diaper changes. Tell your older child that although the baby will need lots of care and attention, he won't really be able to play for some time, and will instead be sleeping and eating a lot so he can grow. When explaining the new baby to your child, be careful not to give her any responsibility. Don't tell her it's "her baby." Tell her the parents will take care of the baby, and that the baby will be an addition to the family, but that she still has a special role and is still a very important part of the family unit.

And don't expect her to understand what you're talking about right away. Your child may seem to ignore you when you talk about the baby; she may look away, talk about something else, or go play with a toy. But all of these tangible activities and discussions will slowly create a schema in her mind of what a baby is, and when your baby arrives, although she may still be surprised, and there will be an adjustment period, she'll have a basic idea of what's happened. Additionally, if you use phrases like "in a few minutes" or "in a little while" for weeks or months prior to the new baby's arrival, your child will become accustomed to waiting. Later, when you have to attend to the new baby's needs first, hearing these words will help your child to be patient.

Moving your child to a new bed or room

Preparing your child for the baby includes some important basic transitions, such as moving her to her new room or new bed, decorating the nursery, and taking out the infant toys. For a young toddler, it's sometimes helpful to make these changes as early as possible so that she doesn't make any connection between this change and the baby's arrival. You don't want her to think she's being kicked out of her crib to make room for the baby. For other children, making the change may be a natural part of sharing the news closer to the baby's arrival.

If you're switching your child to a new bed and she's excited about it, you might take her with you when you shop for the bed (or make a big deal out of thanking the friend or relative who gives you the bed!). She'll love the attention. Buy her a comforter and sheets in a design she loves. If you're moving her to a new room, slowly move all of her items from one room to another. If she'll be sharing a room with the new baby, move her things to one side of the room, slowly, over a period of days. Be prepared for your child to need some extra snuggles at night while she transitions. In the beginning, give her the choice of sleeping in her new space or her old one.

Adjusting to the Arrival of a New Child

Imagine how your child feels when her sibling arrives: She's been the only child for a few years, and now she's got to share her parents' attention with a baby! She may feel angry, resentful, or sad. This is a period of huge adjustment, even if you've made many preparations. It can be very difficult, and the transition can go on for a few months. You may feel as though your older child is handling it perfectly, but then she may (seemingly out of nowhere!) act out, stop listening, or be too rough with the baby. To make things easier, try to complete major changes prior to the baby's arrival. For example, if you're toilet-training your toddler, give her enough time to be comfortable with this new skill before the new baby arrives. (But don't be surprised if she still regresses in this skill.) You don't want her to be focusing on such a big transition while she's also adjusting to her new brother or sister.

Your child's response to the new baby

Often, a child will regress when her new brother or sister arrives. As parents, you should allow her to do the things she hasn't done in months in order to help her feel secure and safe. Perhaps your older child will want to be rocked, or will regress with eating or toileting habits, says the American Academy of Pediatrics. She's doing all this because she's incredibly confused about this major change but also wants to know that she can still get the same amount of love and attention as before. Expect her to be gentle with the baby one minute, but then perhaps too rough the next.

Develop some boundaries for your older child and baby. For instance, tell your older child that she cannot touch the baby when he is nursing or having a bottle. This may be incredibly difficult for your older child, because once she sees that baby nestled in your arms, she'll want to be snuggled in too! So, to make the baby's feeding time fun for your toddler, try a small version of hide-and-seek. Count to 10 and say, "Where are you?" It doesn't matter if your child hides or not; pretend you can't see her. This is especially hilarious if she's standing right in front of you! Ask the baby questions about where she is, and do a silly baby voice answering the questions.

Your older child may also act out, break rules, and try to get any attention, even negative, if it means you have to put the baby down and talk to her. As frustrating as this can be, try to see it from your older child's point of view. Everything in her world has changed, and even though you prepared her, she really had no idea what these changes meant. And she is just a young child, so she cannot communicate these complicated feelings to you. Be patient, give her lots of positive attention, spend time just with her, set boundaries, and continue to "catch her being good." It will take some time, but eventually, this will become her new normal.

Be careful not to use the "big kid" line, because it may anger your child. She doesn't want to be big; she didn't ask for this new addition to the family. She just wants to be small again, to need and receive all the attention that the new baby is getting. Instead, continue to give your older child undivided attention when possible, understanding that she didn't ask for or want this baby, and acknowledge these feelings. When she does act like a "big kid," praise her for her actions, but do not connect it to the baby. For example, "I'm so proud of you for using the toilet! Awesome job!"

Be sure to acknowledge your child's frustrations when you recognize them. For example, if you're going to play outside but the baby needs to nurse first, say, "I know you're frustrated because you want to play outside and the baby has to have some milk, but once he eats, he'll stop crying and I'll be able to focus on our soccer game. So let's feed him, and then we can go outside in a few minutes." Giving exact instructions of what has to happen before you get to go outside will help your older child to conceptualize the next few minutes. (Patience phrases you may have taught her before the baby's arrival, like "in a few minutes," will help her to wait.) Explain the baby's needs in a logical, systematic way, instead of in an emotional way.

Managing sibling rivalry

Much of early sibling rivalry stems from children who feel that their "love cup" is being emptied, as opposed to their sibling's cup, which is always full. For example, your older child may feel that the baby gets lots of love just for sleeping, nursing, and crying. And she may feel that she gets criticized all the time: "Be gentle with the baby! Don't touch!" Combat this by giving your older child specific praises, such as "Great job bringing your plate to the sink!" or, "I love how you built that tower! It's so tall!" Invite her on special outings, and give plenty of hugs, kisses, and affection that will help fill up her heart during this transitional time.

Be very cognizant of spending special, positive time with your older child, even when your infant is awake. For example, if your infant is happily playing in his bouncy chair, use those few minutes to color a picture with your older child, as long as you can keep your infant in your sight. Read her stories at night (and have your partner watch the baby), snuggle with her, do an art project, bake cookies, or even take her out to lunch on a special date. These activities will be crucial to your older child feeling loved at a time where everything around her has changed.

Your older child may at times be rough with the baby, whether this is intentional or not. She could be so excited to have a little brother that she may "smother" him with hugs. To help give both children some space, consider giving each child a special play space that she can call her own.

For example, you might set up some interlocking gates within the family room to create a small, cozy playpen for your infant with developmentally appropriate toys while your toddler has the rest of the room for exploring and playing games or cuddling with her own stuffed animals. This setup enables the children to see and interact with each other but focus on the activities that interest each of them the most—and it keeps them from disturbing each other when a little peace is needed for each!

An older child can help by playing with the infant sibling.

If your child enjoys being helpful, invite her to assist with the baby. Maybe she can get him a diaper, help you to feed him a bottle, or entertain him while you dress him. Some children, while they would love to be helpful, are too young to really help. So make your child feel like part of the process by giving her a task you know she can accomplish well. Just be sure to only assign tasks that she finds fun, because if the tasks are a burden, she may begin to resent the baby's presence.

Naptime and playtime pose special challenges when you have two or more children. We've offered some strategies here, but do look back at Chapter 6, which offers a few more suggestions.

Preparing your child for preschool

You may decide to send your older child to preschool when your new baby arrives. If you make this decision, try to start your child in school before your baby's arrival so she doesn't connect that event with her sibling's arrival. If your older child has already been in full-time child care that mirrors a preschool environment, this transition may not be as dramatic, but it is still a big change, so it needs to be carefully monitored and respected. Begin by reading her books about preschool, and if possible, take her for tours so that she can see what preschool is. Set up a daily schedule in your home that's visually appealing, just like she'll have at school. For example, cut out shapes of various activities such as Breakfast, Outing, Play, and Stories. If your child already goes to a child care facility, the schedule could say Breakfast, Go to School, Home, Play, and Dinner. Attach Velcro to the back and each morning help her to put the activities on a board in the right order. This activity will help her to become comfortable with a predictable schedule.

Begin school slowly, a few days a week, part time, if possible. If she's nervous to leave you, show her as much as you can before the first day. Bring her to the school, have her meet her teacher, and if she already knows another child in class, make a few play dates with that friend. Remind her that you'll be there to pick her up at the end of the day, and be sure not to be late.

Make time each day to discuss her school activities, and invite her to hang her artwork in the house. Talk with her about what she's learning, who her friends are, and her experience with her teacher. When the baby arrives, keep her schedule the same so that she knows that her life is still a priority to you and to the family.

By bringing your child a new sibling, you're creating friends for life. Your care in easing her into her new status as big sister will help reassure her that your love for her hasn't changed. Through this transitional time, be sure to verbally reassure your older child with clear words: "I love you!" or "You don't want to share my time? I understand. I love you and I love your brother. We can all play together." Although it may be a bumpy road at first, know that these difficulties are temporary, and balancing the needs of both your children will get easier.

Activities to Prepare Your Child for a Sibling

Major transitions such as bringing home a new baby can be a major frustration in a young child's life. Although they may be natural to you, to a toddler they may be annoyances that get in the way of her needs and desires. But they are temporary, and your child will find her way out of it. The key is to transition her gently so she continues to feel the love and support you've worked so hard to give her. Note: The following activities can continue even after the new baby arrives!

- Fun new books. Read books about adjusting to new siblings (see sidebar earlier in this chapter).
- "Big brother/big sister" class. In these classes, expectant big brothers and sisters are taught about their role as an older sibling. Often, the teachers stress infant safety, how to hold a baby, and sometimes even how to diaper a baby. You may find this kind of class through your local hospital or religious affiliation.
- Finding other sibling pairs. You can have fun spotting families when you're out in the community. For example, say, "Look! That mommy has two children with her: a boy and a girl. They are brother and sister."
- Baby doll. Buy her a toy baby, and play "house" with it. Imagine the infant needs to be changed, fed, and rocked, and have your child pretend with you as the two of you accomplish these tasks.
- "If you were a baby" game. Say, "If you were a baby and you were hungry, how would you eat? How would you ask for food?" Allow your child to act out these answers if she wants, or just say them aloud.
- Baby book. If your child is an older toddler, encourage her to make a collage or "book" for the baby. She can cut out pictures of things she liked when she was a baby, or you can help her write words and ideas that she thinks the baby needs to know. Phrases like "Don't touch the cat's tail" or "Mom doesn't like it when you throw food on the floor" will help your child feel responsible. Bonus: You'll have an adorable scrapbook to show your children one day!
- Reminiscing. Show your older child photos and videos of her when she was a baby. This is especially useful if you're going to use the same baby equipment. You can show your older child how she used to sit in the bouncy chair and watch the world, just like her baby brother does now.
- Practice for the Big Day! Will your child be staying with grandparents or friends while you're at the hospital or on the adoption trip? Do a practice sleepover. Remind her that you'll see her in the morning (or whenever you will return), and that she will have a special day with her friends or relatives. When you go, remind her that you'll be coming home with the baby. Explain this concept over and over again throughout your pregnancy or waiting period.
- Baby accessories. Take out all of your child's old baby accessories, such as her receiving blankets, pictures, pacifiers, and maybe even some of her small clothes. Talk about why she needed these items, and explain why the baby will need them too. Allow her to pretend with or talk about these items as often as she wants.
- The "love egg." Pretend to crack an egg on your child's head (gently, of course) and glide your hands down her hair as you spread your love through it. This is a great game to continue after your baby arrives.

Conclusion

My hope is that after reading this book, you understand the "whys" behind the games and activities that will help develop your child's cognitive, emotional, and social skills from the age of zero to three. There are lists of games and activities in this book, but it's just as important to allow your child to lead the play and discovery. You may find that some of the best days you have with your young children are the days that you plan nothing and just let them invite you into their world of play.

Be empathetic to his needs. *Make him laugh. Be silly.* Understand that he, like you, needs support, a good listener, a playmate, and someone to love him. He's not trying to make you angry when he cries or screams; he's just trying to communicate in the only way he knows how. Support him and acknowledge his feelings of frustration. If you can't stop what you're doing right then, tell him why. If you're frustrated, tell him you need a few minutes to yourself and then come back to him. Remember that he's always watching you and will copy all of your behaviors. He looks to you to learn how to act when he's angry, sad, happy, or frustrated. If you act in a calm but clear manner, he'll calm down, because he knows you heard him and you respect him, even if he can't have what he wants right this minute.

Be present.

Be consistent.

What a gift it is to be a parent. What a beautiful, incredible gift.

Be there as much as you can. Slow down the time. You have one chance with your children, but you have a new opportunity every day. It's not about every small decision you make, but it is about the overall pattern of love and security that you provide for your child. Even when you make a mistake, forgive yourself and try to handle it better next time. Model imperfection. Explain to your child that we all make mistakes, but that's how we learn. Parenthood is a process. We learn every day. Try to let go of the frustrations and enjoy the sweetness. Having the opportunity at a second childhood is just spectacular, and the years will go by so fast.

–Sarahlynne

Notes

All sources listed in the Notes appear in the Bibliography. Full citations of print sources are given the first time. Online sources are cited in full except the URL, which is included in the Bibliography listing.

Introduction

Decline in marital quality during transition to parenthood and effects on children: G. Rhoades, S. Stanley, and H. Markman, "The Effect of the Transition to Parenthood on Relationship Quality: An 8-Year Prospective Study," *American Psychological Association* 96 (2009), 601–19.

John Medina, *Brain Rules for Baby: How to Raise a Smart and Happy Child from Zero to Five* (Seattle: Pear Press, 2010), 69, 87.

Chapter 1

"Sound mental health, motivation to learn . . . ": National Scientific Council on the Developing Child, "Young Children Develop in an Environment of Relationships," Working Paper No. 1 (2004; updated 2009), 1.

Consistent environments help children in goal-directed behavior: National Scientific Council on the Developing Child, "Building the Brain's 'Air Traffic Control' System: How Early Experiences Shape the Development of Executive Function," Working Paper No. 11 (February 2011), 7.

"Effective interventions can literally alter . . . ": National Scientific Council on the Developing Child, "Early Experiences Can Alter Gene Expression and Affect Long-Term Development," Working Paper No. 10 (May 2010), 2.

Building an early, secure attachment will "contribute to the growth . . . ": National Scientific Council on the Developing Child, "Young Children Develop in an Environment of Relationships," 1.

"We are born with the potential *to develop these capacities . . . ":* National Scientific Council on the Developing Child, "Building the Brain's 'Air Traffic Control' System," 1.

Neurons, synapses, and myelination: Judith Graham, "Children and Brain Development: What We Know about How Children Learn," The University of Maine (2011).

Dennis P. Carmody et al., "A Quantitative Measure of Myelination Development in Infants, Using MR Images," *Neuroradiology* 46, no. 9 (2004), 781–86.

Long-term negative effects of extensive neglect or abuse: John Medina, *Brain Rules for Baby: How to Raise a Smart and Happy Child from Zero to Five* (Seattle: Pear Press, 2010).

Jill Stamm, *Bright from the Start: The Simple, Science-backed Way to Nurture Your Child's Developing Mind from Birth to Age 3* (New York: Gotham Books, 2007), 27.

A Tip from Sarahlynne sidebar, imperfect task completion: John B. Bransford, Ann L. Brown, and Rodney R. Cocking, *How People Learn* (Washington, DC: National Academy Press, 2000), 104.

"Without food or warmth . . . ": Penelope Leach, *Your Baby and Child: From Birth to Age Five*, 3rd edition (New York: Knopf, 2007), 223.

"Having her feelings understood . . . ": Jenn Berman, *SuperBaby: 12 Ways to Give Your Child a Head Start in the First 3 Years* (New York: Sterling Publishing, 2010), 7.

Importance of consistent caregivers: T. Berry Brazelton and Stanley I. Greenspan, *The Irreducible Needs of Children: What Every Child Must Have to Grow, Learn, and Flourish* (Cambridge, MA: Da Capo Press, 2000).

Leach, *Your Baby and Child*, 223.

Importance of quality time to social, cognitive, and intellectual development: Brazelton and Greenspan, *The Irreducible Needs of Children.*

Lawrence Cohen, *Playful Parenting: An Exciting New Approach to Raising Children That Will Help You Nurture Close Connections, Solve Behavior Problems, Encourage Confidence* (New York: Ballantine Books, 2001).

Leach, *Your Baby and Child.*

Recommended 20-minute sessions with baby: Brazelton and Greenspan, *The Irreducible Needs of Children.*

Cohen, *Playful Parenting.*

Chapter 2

What babies learn when parents don't respond: Leach, *Your Baby and Child.*

Dr. Karp and "fourth trimester" strategies: Beth Whitehouse, "Dr. Harvey Karp Explains Why a Newborn Alone in a Quiet Nursery Has Plenty of Reasons to Cry," *The Happiest Baby* (October 2009).

Postpartum depression: Neill Epperson, "Postpartum Major Depression: Detection and Treatment," *American Family Physician* 59, no. 8 (1999), 2247–54.

"Family patterns that undermine nurturing . . . ": Brazelton and Greenspan, *The Irreducible Needs of Children*, 1.

"A child whose cries are consistently responded to in a negative way . . . ": Berman, *SuperBaby*, 33.

Effects of cortisol release on baby's brain and development: William Sears, M.D., and Martha Sears, "Science Says: Excessive Crying Could Be Harmful." AskDrSears.com (2013).

Quotation on "Sensitive, responsive, secure caretaking": Megan R. Gunnar, "Quality of Early Care and Buffering of Neuroendocrine Stress Reactions: Potential Effects on the Developing Human Brain," *Preventive Medicine* 27 (1998), 208–11.

Moro reflex: K. Goldstein, M.D., et al., "Moro Reflex and Startle Pattern," *Archives of Neurology and Psychiatry* 40, no. 2 (1938), 322–27.

"Increased responsiveness to fussing or crying infants lessens the overall amount of infant crying": Joseph Soltis,"The Signal Functions of Early Infant Crying," *Behavioral and Brain Sciences* 27 (2004), 454.

Cry-it-out: Leach, *Your Baby and Child*, 263.

Polly Moore, "Infant Sleep: Answers to Common Questions from Parents," *Consultant for Pediatricians* 8, no. 3 (2009).

Gwen Dewar, "Sleep Training: The Ferber Method and Its Alternatives," *Parenting Science* (2008).

How you respond to your child's tantrums is "one of the greatest predictors . . . ": Medina, *Brain Rules for Baby*, 192.

Bedtime strategies of having baby wait 15 to 20 seconds: Cohen, *Playful Parenting.*

Benefits and techniques of infant massage: Christie Bondurant, "The Benefits of Infant Massage," *Massage Today* 8, no. 3 (2008).

Teresa Kirkpatrick Ramsey, *Baby's First Massage,* 4th edition (Teresa Kirkpatrick Ramsey, 2001).

Berman, *SuperBaby*, 86–89.

Cocoon game activity: Stamm, *Bright from the Start*, 203.

Chapter 3

"An infant studies her parents' faces . . . ": Brazelton and Greenspan, *The Irreducible Needs of Children*, 117.

Problems of powerlessness in tickling: Cohen, *Playful Parenting*, 100.

Benefits of tummy time: Russell Robertson, M.D., "Supine Infant Positioning—Yes, But There's More to It," *Journal of Family Practice* 60, no. 10 (2011), 605–7.

Importance of crawling: M. McEwan, R. Dihoff, and G. Brosvic, "Early Infant Crawling Experience in Later Motor Skill Development," *Perpetual and Motor Skills* 72 (1991), 75–79.

Quotation on corpus callosum: Stamm, *Bright from the Start*, 76–77.

Unsteady toddler won't venture more than 200 feet: Leach, *Your Baby and Child.*

"All of a child's future skills . . . ": Stamm, *Bright from the Start*, 172.

Studies of newborns listening to tunes heard prenatally: Thomas Verny and Pamela R. Weintraub, "The Womb Your Child's First School: How to Provide a Prenatal Environment That Nurtures Your Growing Baby," *Mothering* 132 (2005), 38–43.

Newborns prefer mother's voice: Anthony J. DeCasper and Melanie J. Spence, "Prenatal Maternal Speech Influences Newborns' Perception of Speech Sounds," *Infant Behavior and Development 9* (April–June 1986), 133–50.

Why babies put so many things in their mouths: Kim John Payne, *Simplicity Parenting: Using the Extraordinary Power of Less to Raise Calmer, Happier, and More Secure Kids* (New York: Ballantine Books, 2010), 78.

Failure to thrive and importance of touch: Lisa Cartwright, "Emergencies of Survival: Moral Spectatorship and the 'New Vision of the Child' in Postwar Child Psychoanalysis," *Journal of Visual Culture* 3, no. 1 (2004), 42.

Harry Bakwin, M.D., "Emotional Deprivation in Infants," *Journal of Pediatrics* 35, no. 4 (1949), 512–21.

Chapter 4

Language acquisition begins "in the last trimester . . . ": Betty Bardige and M. Kori Bardige, "Talk to Me, Baby! Supporting Language Development in the First 3 Years," Zero to Three (September 2008), 4.

"Prenatal auditory experience can influence postnatal auditory preferences": DeCasper and Spence, "Prenatal Maternal Speech Influences," 133.

"Adults the world over tend to talk to babies face-to-face, in a high-pitched, singsong . . . ": Bardige and Bardige, "Talk to Me, Baby!" 6.

Study on mothers' and fathers' differing styles of speaking: Nadya Pancsofar and Lynne Vernon-Feagans, "Mother and Father Language Input to Young Children: Contributions to Later Language Development," *Journal of Applied Developmental Psychology* 27 (2006), 583.

The power of play talk: Betty Bardige, personal communication, 2013.

Specific language abilities and number of words infancy to 18 months: Medina, *Brain Rules for Baby*, 129.

Po Bronson and Ashley Merryman, *NurtureShock: New Thinking about Children*, (New York: Hachette, 2009), 218.

K. Beuker et al., "Development of Early Communication Skills in the First Two Years," *Infant Behavior and Development* 36, no. 1 (2013), 72.

Berman, *SuperBaby*, 112.

Impact of parentese on enrollments in gifted and accelerated programs: Medina, *Brain Rules for Baby*, 131.

Rhythmic coupling study: Michael Goldstein and Jennifer Schwade, "Social Feedback to Infants' Babbling Facilitates Rapid Phonological Learning," *Psychological Science* 19, no. 5 (2008), 515–24.

"Children who had heard 33 million words . . . ": Bardige and Bardige, "Talk to Me, Baby!" 5.

The longitudinal studies are described in Betty Hart and Todd R. Risley, *Meaningful Differences in the Everyday Experiences of Young American Children* (Baltimore: Paul H. Brookes, 1995); Betty Hart and Todd R. Risley, *The Social World of Children Learning to Talk* (Baltimore: Paul H. Brookes, 1996).

Cognitive benefits of baby signing: Berman, *SuperBaby*, 119–21.

Fine-motor control, sign language, and verbal language: Medina, *Brain Rules for Baby*, 114.

Benefits for bilingual babies: Kathleen Marcos, "The Benefits of Early Language Learning," Center for Applied Linguistics.

Stamm, *Bright from the Start*, 233.

Chapter 5

"Conventional reading and writing skills . . . ": National Institute for Literacy, "Developing Early Literacy: A Scientific Synthesis of Early Literacy Development and Implications for Interventions," Report of the National Early Literacy Panel (2008).

Importance of repetition for learning English language: James S. Jacobs and Michael O. Tunnell, *Children's Literature Briefly*, 3rd edition (Upper Saddle River, NJ: Pearson, 2004), 24.

Benefits for children who are strong readers and writers: Berman, *SuperBaby*, 178.

Rhode Island hospital study: Wendy S. Masi and Roni Cohen Leiderman, eds., *Gymboree Baby Play: 100 Fun-Filled Activities to Maximize Your Baby's Potential* (San Francisco: Weldon Owen, 2001), 93.

Situated context and distinct literacies: James Paul Gee, *An Introduction to Discourse Analysis: Theory and Method*, 2nd edition (London: Routledge, 2005).

Practice with Cheerios activity: Tonya Wright, "50 Literacy Activities for Babies," *Room to Grow: Making Early Childhood Count* (August 5, 2010).

Finger play activity ("Noble Duke of York"): Wendy S. Masi and Roni Cohen Leiderman, eds., *Gymboree Baby Play: 100 Fun-Filled Activities to Maximize Your Baby's Potential* (San Francisco: Weldon Owen, 2001), 94–95.

Chapter 6

Scaffolding: L. S. Vygotsky, *Mind in Society: The Development of Higher Psychological Processes* (Cambridge, MA: Harvard University Press, 1935/1978).

Play increases creativity and other skills in children and bonding with parents: Regina M. Milteer and Kenneth R. Ginsburg, "The Importance of Play in Promoting Healthy Child Development and Maintaining Strong Parent-Child Bond: Focus on Children in Poverty," *Pediatrics* 129 (January 2012), e204–213.

Positive effects of play on impulse control in three- and four-year-olds: Laura E. Berk, *Awakening Children's Minds: How Parents and Teachers Can Make a Difference* (New York: Oxford University Press, 2001).

Developing curiosity in preschool is vital for the later grades: Joan Almon and Edward Miller, "The Crisis in Early Education: A Research-Based Case for More Play and Less Pressure," *Alliance for Childhood* (November 2011).

Active play can contribute to greater self-esteem: Brazelton and Greenspan, *The Irreducible Needs of Children.*

Parents should "say yes, follow the child's lead . . . ": Cohen, *Playful Parenting*, 160.

What buying too many toys might teach children: Payne, *Simplicity Parenting*, 69.

"Parents who cannot afford these market-driven materials . . . ": Milteer and Ginsburg, "The Importance of Play in Promoting Healthy Child Development," e206.

Electronic toys are too "fixed," don't require problem-solving: Payne, *Simplicity Parenting.*

Eighteen-month-olds can have many toys, but each should be purposeful: Payne, *Simplicity Parenting.*

"Children need time to play with friends outside of formal activities . . . ": Brazelton and Greenspan, *The Irreducible Needs of Children*, 140.

"Toddlers are not old enough to 'fight their own battles' . . . ": Leach, *Your Baby and Child*, 409.

Chapter 7

"Playing what they want to play, how they want to play it . . . ": Cohen, *Playful Parenting*, 158

Small children "use imaginative play and fantasy to take on their fears . . . ": Milteer and Ginsburg, "The Importance of Play in Promoting Healthy Child Development," e206.

Inductive inference: Kim Bilica and Margaret Flores, "Inductive and Deductive Science Thinking: A Model for Lesson Development," *Science Scope* (February 2009), 36–41.

"The creative process involves a letting-go . . . ": Payne, *Simplicity Parenting*, 85.

Kids with formal music instruction have better spatial skills: Katie Overy, "Dyslexia and Music: From Timing Deficits to Musical Interventions," *Annals of the New York Academy of Sciences* 99 (2003), 497–505.

Music will "help children learn to coordinate their movements . . . ": Payne, *Simplicity Parenting*, 86.

McMaster study on infants and music classes: McMaster University, "Babies' Brains Benefit from Music Lessons," Newswise (May 9, 2012).

Tonal adjustment of child singing with parent: Bonnie Brown, Suzuki instructor, personal communication, 2013.

Dr. Dweck's research on praising students: Carol S. Dweck, "Caution—Praise Can Be Dangerous," *American Educator* 23, no. 1 (1999), 4–9.

Quotation on "Putting in effort": Bronson and Merryman, *NurtureShock*, 15.

Chapter 8

Naturalistic intelligence: Howard Gardner, *Intelligence Reframed: Multiple Intelligences for the 21st Century* (New York: Basic Books, 1999).

Nature-deficit disorder: Richard Louv, *Last Child in the Woods: Saving Our Children from Nature-Deficit Disorder* (New York: Algonquin Books, 2008), 7.

Michael Bentley, "Nature Deficit Disorder: A Plague on Our House," Education.com (2009).

"Stress levels . . . are positively affected by time spent in nature": Richard Louv, "A Walk in the Woods: Right or Privilege?" *Orion* (March/April 2009).

Being idle "allows the circuitry to develop . . . ": Stamm, *Bright from the Start*, 106.

"The womb is louder than a vacuum cleaner . . . ": Harvey Karp (interviewee) and NPR Staff (interviewer), "Dr. Karp on Parenting and the Science of Sleep," NPR.org interview transcript (June 24, 2012).

Chapter 9

Two-thirds of infants and toddlers average two hours of screen time daily: Kidshealth.org, "How TV Affects Your Child," reviewed by Dr. Steven Dowhen (October 2011).

AAP guidelines on TV time for toddlers: American Academy of Pediatrics, "Policy Statement: Media Use by Children Younger Than 2 Years," *Pediatrics* 128, no. 5 (October 17, 2011), 1040–45.

Newborns' visual abilities and limitations: Daniel R. Anderson and Katherine G. Hanson, "From Blooming, Buzzing Confusion to Media Literacy: The Early Development of Television Viewing," *Developmental Review* 30 (2010), 239–55.

Early TV viewing and ADHD: Dimitri A. Christakis et al., "Early Television Exposure and Subsequent Attentional Problems in Children," *Pediatrics* 113 (2004), 710.

Report on other researchers' attempts to replicate the study: Mary L. Courage and Mark L. Howe, "To Watch or Not to Watch: Infants and Toddlers in a Brave New Electronic World," *Developmental Review* 30, no. 2 (2010), 101–115.

ADD/ADHD may be correlated with early TV watching: Kidshealth.org, "What Is ADHD?" reviewed by Dr. Richard S. Kingsley (January 2012).

Quotation on "Children with a parent-reported ADHD diagnosis . . . ": Centers for Disease Control and Prevention, "Attention-Deficit/Hyperactivity Disorder Data and Statistics in the United States," CDC Home (December 2011).

Effects of constant TV household: Ellen Wartella, "The Influence of Media on Young Children's Development," Zero to Three (January 2012), 19.

Advertisers spend millions marketing to young children: Payne, *Simplicity Parenting*, 58.

"97% of American children six or under have [toy] products based on TV . . . ": Payne, *Simplicity Parenting*, 58, citing Victoria J. Rideout, Elizabeth J. Vandewater, and Ellen Wartella, *Zero to Six: Electronic Media in the Lives of Infants, Toddlers, and Preschoolers* (Menlo Park, CA: Henry J. Kaiser Family Foundation, 2003), 4.

TV and media marketers teaching children to be unhappy with what they have: Mary Pipher, *The Shelter of Each Other: Rebuilding Our Families* (New York: Putnam, 1996), 56, 93.

Two-year study of preschoolers watching so-called educational programs: Jamie M. Ostrov, Douglas A. Gentile, and Nikki R. Crick, "Media Exposure, Aggression, and Prosocial Behavior during Early Childhood: A Longitudinal Study," *Social Development* 15, no. 4 (2006), 612–27.

Bronson and Merryman, *NurtureShock.*

"For every hour per day the children spent watching certain baby DVDs and videos . . . ": Medina, *Brain Rules for Baby*, 148.

University of Washington study of media exposure and language development: Frederick J. Zimmerman, Dimitri A. Christakis, and Andrew N. Meltzoff, "Associations between Media Viewing and Language Development in Children under Age 2 Years," *Journal of Pediatrics* 10, no. 4 (October 2007), 364–68.

When kids watch too much, they "miss out on the give-and-take . . . ": Brazelton and Greenspan, *The Irreducible Needs of Children*, 128.

Chapter 10

Best friends prepare children for siblinghood: Laurie Kramer and John M. Gottman, "Becoming a Sibling: 'With a Little Help from My Friends,'" *Developmental Psychology* 28, no. 4 (1992), 695.

Talking with a toddler about the new baby a few months before arrival: American Academy of Pediatrics, "Preparing Your Family for a New Baby," Healthychildren.org (January 2, 2013).

Leach, *Your Baby and Child*, 409.

Regression of eating and toilet training when new baby arrives: American Academy of Pediatrics, "Preparing Your Family for a New Baby," Healthychildren.org (January 2, 2013).

Toddler with baby sibling may feel constantly criticized: Cohen, *Playful Parenting.*

The "love egg" activity: Cohen, *Playful Parenting*, 24.

Bibliography

Almon, Joan, and Edward Miller. "The Crisis in Early Education: A Research-Based Case for More Play and Less Pressure." Alliance for Childhood (November 2011). www.allianceforchildhood.org.

American Academy of Pediatrics. "Policy Statement: Media Use by Children Younger Than 2 Years." *Pediatrics* 128, no. 5 (October 17, 2011): 1040–45. doi:10.1542/peds.2011-1753. http://pediatrics.aappublications.org/content/early/2011/10/12/peds.2011-1753.full.pdf+html

American Academy of Pediatrics. "Preparing Your Family for a New Baby." Healthychildren.org. Last updated January 2, 2013. http://www.healthychildren.org/English/family-life/family-dynamics/Pages/Preparing-Your-Family-for-a-New-Baby.aspx

American Academy of Pediatrics. "SIDS and Other Sleep-Related Infant Deaths: Expansion of Recommendations for a Safe Infant Sleeping Environment." *Pediatrics* 10 (October 17, 2011): 1542/peds. 2011–84. doi:10.1542/peds.2011-2284.

Anderson, Daniel R., and Katherine G. Hanson. "From Blooming, Buzzing Confusion to Media Literacy: The Early Development of Television Viewing." *Developmental Review* 30 (2010): 239–55.

Bakwin, Harry, M.D. "Emotional Deprivation in Infants." *Journal of Pediatrics* 35, no. 4 (1949): 512–21.

Bardige, Betty, and M. Kori Bardige. "Talk to Me, Baby! Supporting Language Development in the First 3 Years." Zero to Three (September 2008): 4–10. http://www.zerotothree.org

Bentley, Michael. "Nature Deficit Disorder: A Plague on Our House." Education.com (2009). http://www.education.com/reference/article/nature-deficit-disorder-plague-our-house/

Berk, Laura E. *Awakening Children's Minds: How Parents and Teachers Can Make a Difference*. New York: Oxford University Press, 2001.

Berman, Jenn. *SuperBaby: 12 Ways to Give Your Child a Head Start in the First 3 Years*. New York: Sterling Publishing, 2010.

Beuker, K., N. Rommelse, R. Donders, and J. Buitelaar. "Development of Early Communication Skills in the First Two Years." *Infant Behavior and Development* 36, no. 1 (2013): 71–83.

Bilica, Kim, and Margaret Flores. "Inductive and Deductive Science Thinking: A Model for Lesson Development." *Science Scope* (February 2009): 36–41. http://esc.tricountyesc.org/cos/scienceresources/9-Article-Inductive-Deductive-Science-Thinking-A-Model-for-Lesson-Development.pdf

Bondurant, Christie. "The Benefits of Infant Massage." *Massage Today* 8, no. 3 (2008).

Bransford, John B., Ann L. Brown, and Rodney R. Cocking. *How People Learn*. Washington, DC: National Academy Press, 2000.

Brazelton, T. Berry, and Stanley I. Greenspan. *The Irreducible Needs of Children: What Every Child Must Have to Grow, Learn, and Flourish*. Cambridge, MA: Da Capo Press, 2000.

Bronson, Po, and Ashley Merryman. *NurtureShock: New Thinking about Children*. New York: Hachette, 2009.

Carmody, Dennis P., Stanley M. Dunn, Akiza S. Boddie-Willis, J. Kevin DeMarco, and Michael Lewis. "A Quantitative Measure of Myelination Development in Infants, Using MR Images." *Neuroradiology* 46, no. 9 (2004): 781–86.

Cartwright, Lisa. "Emergencies of Survival: Moral Spectatorship and the 'New Vision of the Child' in Postwar Child Psychoanalysis." *Journal of Visual Culture* 3, no. 1 (2004): 35–49.

Centers for Disease Control and Prevention. "Attention-Deficit/Hyperactivity Disorder Data and Statistics in the United States." CDC Home (December 2011). http://www.cdc.gov/ncbddd/adhd/data.html

Christakis, Dimitri A., Frederick J. Zimmerman, David L. DiGiuseppe, and Carolyn A. McCarty. "Early Television Exposure and Subsequent Attentional Problems in Children." *Pediatrics* 113 (2004): 708–14.

Codell, Esmé Raji. *How to Get Your Child to Love Reading: For Ravenous and Reluctant Readers Alike.* New York: Workman Publishing, 2003.

Cohen, Lawrence J. *Playful Parenting: An Exciting New Approach to Raising Children That Will Help You Nurture Close Connections, Solve Behavior Problems, Encourage Confidence.* New York: Ballantine Books, 2001.

Courage, Mary L., and Mark L. Howe. "To Watch or Not to Watch: Infants and Toddlers in a Brave New Electronic World." *Developmental Review* 30, no. 2 (2010): 101–115.

DeCasper, Anthony J., and Melanie J. Spence. "Prenatal Maternal Speech Influences Newborns' Perception of Speech Sounds." *Infant Behavior and Development* 9 (April–June 1986): 133–50.

Dewar, Gwen. "Sleep Training: The Ferber Method and Its Alternatives." *Parenting Science* (2008). http://www.parentingscience.com/Ferber-method.html

Dweck, Carol S. "Caution—Praise Can Be Dangerous." *American Educator* 23, no. 1 (1999): 4–9.

Epperson, Neill. "Postpartum Major Depression: Detection and Treatment." *American Family Physician* 59, no. 8 (1999): 2247–54. http://www.aafp.org/afp/1999/0415/p2247.html

Gardner, Howard. *Intelligence Reframed: Multiple Intelligences for the 21st Century.* New York: Basic Books, 1999.

Gee, James Paul. *An Introduction to Discourse Analysis: Theory and Method.* 2nd edition. London: Routledge, 2005.

Goldstein, K., M.D., C. Landis, W. A. Hunt, and F. Clark. "Moro Reflex and Startle Pattern." *Archives of Neurology and Psychiatry* 40, no. 2 (1938): 322–27.

Goldstein, Michael, and Jennifer Schwade. "Social Feedback to Infants' Babbling Facilitates Rapid Phonological Learning." *Psychological Science* 19, no. 5 (2008): 515–24.

Graham, Judith. "Children and Brain Development: What We Know about How Children Learn." The University of Maine (2011). http://umaine.edu/publications/4356e/

Gunnar, Megan R. "Quality of Early Care and Buffering of Neuroendocrine Stress Reactions: Potential Effects on the Developing Human Brain." *Preventive Medicine* 27 (1998): 208–11.

Hart, Betty, and Todd R. Risley. *Meaningful Differences in the Everyday Experiences of Young American Children.* Baltimore: Paul H. Brookes, 1995.

Hart, Betty, and Todd R. Risley. *The Social World of Children Learning to Talk.* Baltimore: Paul H. Brookes, 1999.

Jacobs, James S., and Michael O. Tunnell. *Children's Literature Briefly.* 3rd edition. Upper Saddle River, NJ: Pearson, 2004.

Karp, Harvey (interviewee), and NPR Staff (interviewer). "Dr. Karp on Parenting and the Science of Sleep." NPR.org interview transcript (June 24, 2012). http://www.npr.org/2012/06/24/155426534/dr-karp-on-parenting-and-the-science-of-sleep

Kidshealth.org. "How TV Affects Your Child." Reviewed by Dr. Steven Dowhen (October 2011). http://kidshealth.org/parent/positive/family/tv_affects_child.html

Kidshealth.org. "What Is ADHD?" Reviewed by Dr. Richard S. Kingsley (January 2012). http://kidshealth.org/parent/emotions/behavior/adhd.html#

Kramer, Laurie, and John M. Gottman. "Becoming a Sibling: 'With a Little Help from My Friends.'" *Developmental Psychology* 28, no. 4 (1992): 685–99.

Leach, Penelope. *Your Baby and Child: From Birth to Age Five.* 3rd edition. New York: Knopf, 2007.

Louv, Richard. *Last Child in the Woods: Saving Our Children from Nature-Deficit Disorder.* New York: Algonquin Books, 2008.

Louv, Richard. "A Walk in the Woods: Right or Privilege?" *Orion* (March/April 2009). http://www.orionmagazine.org/index.php/articles/article/4401

Marcos, Kathleen. "The Benefits of Early Language Learning." Center for Applied Linguistics. http://www.cal.org/resources/archive/rgos/benes.html

Masi, Wendy S., and Roni Cohen Leiderman, eds. *Gymboree Baby Play: 100 Fun-Filled Activities to Maximize Your Baby's Potential.* San Francisco: Weldon Owen, 2001.

McEwan, M., R. Dihoff, and G. Brosvic. "Early Infant Crawling Experience in Later Motor Skill Development." *Perpetual and Motor Skills* 72 (1991): 75–79.

McMaster University. "Babies' Brains Benefit from Music Lessons." Newswise (May 9, 2012). http://www.newswise.com/articles/babies-brains-benefit-from-music-lessons

Medina, John. *Brain Rules for Baby: How to Raise a Smart and Happy Child from Zero to Five.* Seattle: Pear Press, 2010.

Milteer, Regina M., and Kenneth R. Ginsburg. "The Importance of Play in Promoting Healthy Child Development and Maintaining Strong Parent-Child Bond: Focus on Children in Poverty." *Pediatrics* 129 (January 2012): 204–13. doi:10.1542/peds.2011-2953

Moore, Polly. "Infant Sleep: Answers to Common Questions from Parents." *Consultant for Pediatricians* 8, no. 3 (2009).

National Institute for Literacy. "Developing Early Literacy: A Scientific Synthesis of Early Literacy Development and Implications for Interventions." Report of the National Early Literacy Panel (2008). http://lincs.ed.gov/publications/pdf/NELPReport09.pdf

National Research Council. *How People Learn: Brain, Mind, Experiences, and School.* Washington, DC: National Academy Press, 2000.

National Scientific Council on the Developing Child. "Building the Brain's 'Air Traffic Control' System: How Early Experiences Shape the Development of Executive Function." Working Paper No. 11 (February 2011): 1–17. http://www.developingchild.harvard.edu

National Scientific Council on the Developing Child. "Early Experiences Can Alter Gene Expression and Affect Long-Term Development." Working Paper No. 10 (May 2010): 1–9. http://www.developingchild.net

National Scientific Council on the Developing Child. "Young Children Develop in an Environment of Relationships." Working Paper No. 1 (2004; updated 2009): 1–8. http://www.developingchild.net

Ostrov, Jamie M., Douglas A. Gentile, and Nikki R. Crick. "Media Exposure, Aggression, and Prosocial Behavior during Early Childhood: A Longitudinal Study." *Social Development* 15, no. 4 (2006): 612–27.

Overy, Katie. "Dyslexia and Music: From Timing Deficits to Musical Interventions." *Annals of the New York Academy of Sciences* 99 (2003): 497–505.

Pancsofar, Nadya, and Lynne Vernon-Feagans. "Mother and Father Language Input to Young Children: Contributions to Later Language Development." *Journal of Applied Developmental Psychology* 27 (2006): 571–87.

Payne, Kim John. *Simplicity Parenting: Using the Extraordinary Power of Less to Raise Calmer, Happier, and More Secure Kids.* New York: Ballantine Books, 2010.

Pipher, Mary. *The Shelter of Each Other: Rebuilding Our Families.* New York: Putnam, 1996.

Ramsey, Teresa Kirkpatrick. *Baby's First Massage.* 4th edition. Teresa Kirkpatrick Ramsey, 2001.

Reynolds, Cecil. "Intelligence Testing." Education.com (2003–2009). http://www.education.com/reference/article/intelligence-testing/

Rhoades, G., S. Stanley, and H. Markman. "The Effect of the Transition to Parenthood on Relationship Quality: An 8-Year Prospective Study." *American Psychological Association* 96 (2009): 601–19.

Rideout, Victoria J., Elizabeth J. Vandewater, and Ellen Wartella. *Zero to Six: Electronic Media in the Lives of Infants, Toddlers, and Preschoolers.* Menlo Park, CA: Henry J. Kaiser Family Foundation, 2003.

Robertson, Russell, M.D. "Supine Infant Positioning—Yes, But There's More to It." *Journal of Family Practice* 60, no. 10 (2011): 605–7.

Sarason, Seymour B. *And What Do You Mean by Learning?* Portsmouth, NH: Heinemann, 2004.

Sears, William, M.D., and Martha Sears. "Science Says: Excessive Crying Could Be Harmful." Ask Dr. Sears.com (2013). http://www.askdrsears.com/topics/fussy-baby/science-says-excessive-crying-could-be-harmful

Soltis, Joseph. "The Signal Functions of Early Infant Crying." *Behavioral and Brain Sciences* 27 (2004): 443–90.

Stamm, Jill. *Bright from the Start: The Simple, Science-Backed Way to Nurture Your Child's Developing Mind from Birth to Age 3*. New York: Gotham Books, 2007.

Verny, Thomas, and Pamela R. Weintraub. "The Womb Your Child's First School: How to Provide a Prenatal Environment That Nurtures Your Growing Baby." *Mothering* 132 (2005): 38–43.

Vygotsky, L. S. *Mind in Society: The Development of Higher Psychological Processes*. Cambridge, MA: Harvard University Press, 1935/1978.

Wartella, Ellen. "The Influence of Media on Young Children's Development." Zero to Three (January 2012): 18–21. http://www.zerotothree.org

What to Expect. "Milestones to Walking." Accessed February 20, 2013. http://www.whattoexpect.com/toddler-walking-milestones.aspx

Whitehouse, Beth. "Dr. Harvey Karp Explains Why a Newborn Alone in a Quiet Nursery Has Plenty of Reasons to Cry." The Happiest Baby (October 2009). http://www.happiestbaby.com/why-newborn-has-plenty-of-reasons-to-cry/

Wright, Tonya. "50 Literacy Activities for Babies." Room to Grow: Making Early Childhood Count (August 5, 2010). http://earlyliteracycounts.blogspot.com/2010/08/50-literacy-activities-for-babies.html

Zimmerman, Frederick J., Dimitri A. Christakis, and Andrew N. Meltzoff. "Associations between Media Viewing and Language Development in Children under Age 2 Years." *Journal of Pediatrics* 10, no. 4 (October 2007): 364–68.

More great books from the *What Now?* Series!

Lesson Ladder is dedicated to helping you prepare for life's most fundamental challenges. We provide practical tools and well-rounded advice that help you achieve your goals while climbing the personal or professional ladder—whether it is preparing to start a family of your own, getting your child potty trained, or learning a new kind of financial management.

I'm Having a Baby! Well-Rounded Perspectives

Collective wisdom for a more comforting and "balanced" understanding of what to expect during pregnancy, childbirth, and the days that follow. $16.99

I Had My Baby! A Pediatrician's Essential Guide to the First 6 Months

Gain confidence to experience the true joy of parenthood! From learning what to expect during those first minutes in the hospital through your baby's first 6 months, this concise, reader-friendly, and reassuring guide covers core topics you'll need to know as a new parent. $16.99

I'm Potty Training My Child: Proven Methods That Work

Respecting that children and parenting styles differ, we created this guide to offer a variety of effective training solutions to help today's busy parents with easy, fast reading, and even faster results! $12.99

Better Behavior for Ages 2–10: Small Miracles That Work Like Magic

For the harried parent, this book offers the compassion, help, and proven solutions you need to manage—and prevent—difficult child behavior. $16.99

Call toll-free to order! **1-800-301-4647**
Or order online: **www.LessonLadder.com**

CPSIA information can be obtained at www.ICGtesting.com
Printed in the USA
LVOW02s1539201014

409615LV00011B/43/P

9 780984 865789